Own Your Space
Keep Yourself and Your Stuff Safe Online

Linda McCarthy

♦Addison-Wesley

Upper Saddle River, NJ • Boston • Indianapolis • San Francisco
New York • Toronto • Montreal • London • Munich • Paris • Madrid
Cape Town • Sydney • Tokyo • Singapore • Mexico City

Publisher Symantec Press: Linda McCarthy
Editor in Chief: Karen Gettman
Acquisitions Editor: Jessica W. Goldstein
Managing Editor: Gina Kanouse
Cover Designer: Alan Clements
Cover Artist: Mirana Reviere
Interior Artists: Ben Gibson and Stickman Studios
Project Editor: Christy Hackerd
Copy Editor: Bart Reed
Indexer: Erika Millen
Proofreader: Debbie Williams
Compositor: Kim Scott, Bumpy Design
Manufacturing Buyer: Dan Uhrig

The publisher offers excellent discounts on this book when ordered in quantity for bulk purchases or special sales, which may include electronic versions and/or custom covers and content particular to your business, training goals, marketing focus, and branding interests. For more information, please contact:

U. S. Corporate and Government Sales
(800) 382-3419
corpsales@pearsontechgroup.com

For sales outside the U. S., please contact:

International Sales
international@pearsoned.com

Visit us on the Web: www.awprofessional.com

ISBN 0-321-42642-8
Text printed in the United States on recycled paper at Edwards Brothers, Inc., in Ann Arbor, Michigan.
Third printing, January 2007

Library of Congress Cataloging-in-Publication Data

McCarthy, Linda.

 Own your space : keep yourself and your stuff safe online / Linda McCarthy.

   p. cm.

 ISBN 0-321-42642-8 (pbk. : alk. paper) 1. Computer security. 2. Computers and children. 3. Internet and teenagers. 4. Computer networks--Security measures. I. Title.

QA76.9.A25.M4 2006

005.8--dc22

                         2006023461

To my digital family.

Table of Contents

Acknowledgments

I would like to offer a special thanks to my editor Denise Weldon-Siviy, for her solid research, detailed suggestions, and support. And to her children—Tabitha, Nina, Kayla, and Nathan—who graciously downloaded worms, accepted viruses, and unknowingly installed pernicious Adware, unwittingly preparing her to provide another parental perspective for this book.

Next, I thank my family, especially Gordon for his great suggestions, help creating the title, and for giving me the space to work many weekends and nights to get this book to press, and Douglas and Eric, two very smart, creative teenagers on our home network who demonstrated how easy it was to destroy a secure home network simply by using the Internet the way teens do. Without their influence I would never have written this book.

At Addison-Wesley, I would like to thank Jessica Goldstein, one of the best editors I have had the opportunity to work with, and Chanda Leary, for all her great marketing support and suggestions. Finally, I would like to thank Christy Hackerd for keeping all the moving parts moving, and Eric Garulay for his great artistic influence.

A special thanks for the teens who reviewed this book—Dan Federman, David Benjamin, and the rest of the teens and security experts selected by Addison-Wesley, Steve Johnson, Trina Helson, Audrey Doyle, Kirby Kuehl, and Rick Kingslan.

I would also like to thank Ollie Whitehouse and Davis Weatherby for suggestions and help with the wireless section, and Sarah Gordon for her suggestions in the malicious code section.

About the Author

Linda McCarthy is an architect in the office of the CTO at Symantec. Linda started her security career breaking into computers on Sun Microsystems' network over a decade ago. Linda has broken into systems around the world to show executives how easy it was to break into their networks. Linda was the vice president of Systems Engineering for Recourse Technologies and is founder of Network Defense.

Linda has published seven books on computer security, and is the author of *IT Security Risking the Corporation*. Linda also received the Woman of Influence Award for computer security, a prestigious award given annually to only four women in the world.

Preface

I was inspired to write *Own Your Space* when the two teenagers in **MY** house managed to destroy what I thought was a pretty darn secure home computer network. I was more inspired when I realized that Douglas and Eric weren't looking to break things or even trying to impress me when they brought down systems on our network. They were just using the Internet the way normal teenagers do.

After that, I started keeping a closer eye on the boys' online lives. I noticed that unlike many adults I know, the boys were hyperaware of things such as low bandwidth and slowing connection speeds. While they weren't yet aware that those symptoms often reflected an infestation of adware or malicious code, they were astoundingly tuned in to even minor changes in their online capabilities. It occurred to me that nowhere would I find an audience more in need of computer security advice. Even better, nowhere would I find an audience more likely to not only understand but actually implement proper security measures. After all, the boys weren't protecting anything as esoteric as critical corporate data. This was a major part of their social lives—something REALLY important.

Who This Book Is For

This is a book for every teen and is an essential resource for every parent. Especially though, this is a book for the computer-savvy, keyboard-comfy teens who use the Net every day and want to know how to secure their systems, lifestyles on the Net, and their data. This book provides important details to keep those teens, their privacy, and their identities safe in cyberspace.

This is a book for normal teenagers like you. I realize that you understand quite a bit about computers, probably a lot more than your parents. I also know from my own teens where the gaps in your computer knowledge tend to fall. I've written this book to address those gaps.

Because I know your time is limited, I've kept it short and tried to focus on the important aspects of security. I've also included examples and case studies of real teenagers just like you.

Even if you're a power user, this book is still for you! Sure, you'll know a number of the details I'll be covering. Still, I'm willing to bet that you'll find a number of details you weren't aware of before. And you'll certainly find a lot of detailed information you should share with a less enlightened friend, sibling, or parent. Therefore, if you already know everything in this book, please pass it to your parents!

Who This Book Is Still For, Just Not Quite 100% For

You'll find that while this is a book full of details, it isn't a book full of numbered instructions, and I tried to keep screenshots to a minimum. I wanted to write a book you would want to sit down and read, not another 400-page technical manual filled with screenshots. To any Mac users, I apologize for including only screenshots based on Microsoft XP. Much as I wanted to include all variations, I didn't want to stress the seams on your backpack in the process. Still, **80% of this book applies every bit as much to Mac users as everyone else.**

As you're reading through, keep that in mind. Hackers tend not to target Macs as often as PCs, but when they do the results are every bit as annoying and potentially devastating. However, expect the bad guys to start targeting Macs simply because they can as that platform continues to expand. Therefore, Mac users need to follow the same security procedures—installing firewalls, updating antivirus software, and so on. You simply need to do so using software designed for the Mac.

What You'll Learn

This book is designed for any teen who is:

- In fear of drive-by downloads of nasty adware, spyware, and viruses

- Trying to stay safe on MySpace

- Worried about online predators and identity thieves

- Scattering secrets to the wind in favorite hotspots

- Shopping online without protecting parental credit card and financial data

- Blogging alone and in the dark

Need to know about these topics? If you're online at any time, you bet you do.

Chapter 1

Know Your Villains

Ed: The Slow-Motion Commander

Meet Ed, a 13-year-old boy from McKeesport, Pennsylvania who enjoys online games. Ed was spending his summer with his aunt in Gettysburg and had been waiting weeks for his new computer to arrive. He connected his computer to the Internet as soon as he unpacked it, surfed the Web a little, and then logged into his favorite game site. After surfing the Web and playing *Commando* for three days, his brand-new computer had gone from supersonic speed to dead in the water. The machine was so slow, it was unusable. After getting no help from tech support, Ed's uncle helped him pack up the computer and send it back. So much for a high-tech summer vacation.

What happened? Like so many of your peers, Ed had a rather nasty introduction to the concept of malicious code. The "nasty code" that killed Ed's new computer was probably spyware or unwanted adware. Like many teens, Ed connected his new PC out of the box without installing any security. It's just a matter of time before a system without security installed that's connected to the Internet slows down to the point of becoming useless. For gamers like Ed, it can happen in only a few hours.

Unlike the case of computer viruses, a lot of people don't know much about how adware gets installed on their computers. Even fewer know about spyware, drive-by downloads, P2P security issues, or EULA-piggybacked Trojans.

Unfortunately, a lot of teens really need to know. Since the Internet's inception in the late 1970s, the number of people who use the Net has doubled every 9 to 14 months. Do the math and you'll see a phenomenal growth chart—from 281 computers on the Internet in 1981 to a dazzling 400 million in 2000. By 2010, worldwide usage is expected to pass 1 billion netizens. Internet usage in the U.S. is nearing saturation levels.

Netizen A citizen of cyberspace (i.e., the Internet). A netizen is any person using the Internet to participate in online social communities. When you add another IM address to your Buddy list, you are expanding your online social group. You are, in effect, being a good netizen!

While Internet usage among adults has risen steadily, Internet usage among teenagers has soared. As of 2005, over half of your peers, an astonishing 19 million, lived in homes with Internet connections.[1]

As you'll learn later, your computer is a special risk. Adware sites target teenagers just like you by focusing their efforts on websites you and your peers tend to visit. Online forums are targeted by pedophiles posing as teens. Even identity theft, another potential consequence of nasty code, can be especially nasty for teenagers still in the process of defining their financial and business identities. If you use your parents' computers, you may also put their financial and personal information at risk.

---

1. Even more important, they made heavy use of the technology. In 2005, roughly two-thirds of American adults were using the Internet. The same year, however, 87% of teens used the Internet—fully half of those going online at least once a day.

For now, just keep in mind that there's a lot more to Internet security than running antivirus software. And, it's a lot more important than you probably realize at this point. Over the next few chapters, I'll be talking about what you need to know and do to help keep yourself, your computer, and maybe even your parents safer when using the Internet.

1.1 A Survey of Bad Code

Malicious code is a piece of programming code specifically developed to harm a computer or its data. **Malware** is a generic term for malicious code. If you've studied Spanish (or Latin, for that matter), you'll know that *mal* simply means "bad"—as in malcontent (a discontented, unhappy person), maladroit (a clumsy, not at all adroit person), and Darth Maul in *Star Wars: Episode I* (the obvious bad guy dressed in red and sporting horns). Nothing good ever starts with "mal." Malware is, quite literally, bad software.

Malware   Programming code designed to harm a computer or its data.

Since malicious code and malware mean the same thing, for simplicity sake I will use the term *malicious code* throughout this book.

In the world of malicious code, there are several standard types of villains. We'll be covering all of these villains throughout the book, but the main categories are:

- Viruses
- Worms
- Trojans
- Bot armies
- Keystroke loggers
- Spyware
- Adware

You're probably already familiar with some of these categories. For instance, computer viruses are now so well-known in the popular culture that they provided the grand finale to the 1996 sci-fi thriller *Independence Day*. If you'll recall, Will Smith saved the day by helping Jeff Goldblum (better known as Ian Malcolm of *Jurassic Park*) to upload a computer virus to the "mother ship," disabling the alien space crafts' force fields. In real life, viruses and worms have taken out entire unprotected networks. For example, in January 2003 the SQL Slammer worm disrupted 13,000 ATMs on the Bank of America's network.

You are no doubt also familiar with antivirus software. Most, but not all, new computers now arrive fresh from the factory already preloaded with at least a trial version of one of the major antivirus packages. Usually, that's Norton AntiVirus or McAfee. For virus protection, both are excellent products.

You may not be aware, however, that some antivirus software will *not* protect you against *all* types of malicious code. Many people think as long as they have antivirus software installed that they are safe from attack. That's not true because several layers of security are needed to protect you. Antivirus software is only one of those layers.

Before we take a look at the other layers of security, it is important to understand what antivirus software can and cannot do. Think of your antivirus software as a series of vaccinations. Having a polio vaccination won't keep you from getting hepatitis. Likewise, having antivirus software won't necessarily protect your computer from spyware or adware.

In fact, if you don't routinely update your antivirus software, it may not even protect you from viruses. Like their biological cousins, computer viruses mutate, and do so quickly. Just as you may need a new flu shot each winter to protect against new viral strands, you also need to update your antivirus software continuously. For other types of malicious code, you may need other types of protection. I'll explain these as we discuss the specific types of malicious code.

1.2 Protect Your Turf, Then Surf!

When you buy a computer, it is not secure. You should never pull a computer out of the box and connect it to the Internet unless you take steps to protect it. Think of your PC as a world traveler who needs vaccinations to avoid diseases in its travels.

In fact, your new computer most likely is plagued with numerous **security holes**, which are flaws in the way your computer's programs have been written that would make your computer vulnerable to attack. Just how serious the flaws in the code are determines how much access an attacker or that attacker's malicious code can gain.

> **Warning!**
>
> Uneducated programmers + programming mistakes = security holes!

If you're wondering why your computer has holes before you use it, the answer is that computer systems run on programs—seemingly endless lines of code that tell the computer how to interpret what you, the user, want to do. Windows XP, a widely used operating system, contains 50 million lines of code. Those lines tell the computer what to do when you drag an unwanted file to the Recycle bin or ask Microsoft Outlook to go to the Internet and see whether anyone has sent you new email. All those lines of code are written by human programmers. Sometimes those programmers simply make mistakes. These programming errors can sometimes be leveraged by attacks to gain unauthorized access to your computer. I know this sounds strange, but most programmers were never taught how to write secure code. To take it one step further, programmers don't think like criminals. I don't use that term very often, but that's what someone who deliberately steals or damages someone else's data is—a criminal. Your average programmer hasn't always thought, "Gee, I could use these lines of code to break into the user's system," because the programmer doesn't actually WANT to break into the user's system.

Security Hole   Any flaw in the way a computer program is written or used that makes your computer vulnerable to attack. Security experts also call this a security vulnerability.

The lack of focus on security as part of the design process is starting to change. More programmers are beginning to audit their code with special tools that look for programming errors that can lead to unauthorized access to the system or data. It will take a long time for the programming community to catch up, however. Think of the millions of lines of code already out there that have been developed by programmers with good intent, but poor security-programming skills. Since all computer systems have security holes, you must protect yourself and patch those holes *before you start surfing the Internet, downloading music, or gaming.*

> **Warning!**
>
> Once connected to the Internet, an unprotected PC can fall victim to an attack in as little as 30 seconds! Protect your PC before you surf!

Why so fast? Once you're online, it can take as little as 30 seconds for someone to attack your machine. If you don't install security first, that first attacker may gain access to your computer without you even knowing about it! At best, your machine may slow down, as Ed's did in the earlier example. At worst, the attacker could make off with enough personal data to steal your identity. If you use financial software to track the bank account you opened for college savings when you picked up that after-school job, keep in mind that your data isn't just information. It could be cash as well. And just to add another twist, a hacker could even use your computer to launch an attack on other computers! For these reasons (and many more I'll get to later), don't ever surf the Internet without security patches, antivirus software, and a firewall installed. *A firewall is a piece of software that controls the type of traffic that is allowed to pass between two networks (covered in detail in Chapter 11, "Any Port in a Storm").*

Products to Purchase:
Anti-Virus
Anti-Spyware
Personal Firewall
Security Patches

When you bought your computer, I'll bet you started with a list of requirements: how much memory, how much disk space, what kind of graphics you'd need for your favorite games, whether you want to burn DVDs as well as view them. Before you go online, you also need a Computer Security shopping list. This list is a basic list. You should not leave any one of those items off your list. Virus protection **must** be on that list. You have to install it and configure it to update your computer automatically. You also need to purchase software to protect against spyware and adware. Sometimes, you can buy this bundled with antivirus software. But check. Not all antivirus software includes this protection. Make sure that yours does! You also need to install any security patches that have been issued for the operating system and the browser you plan to use.

Security Patch A fix to a program to close a known security hole. Patches are routinely issued for operating systems (such as Windows XP) and Internet browsers (such as Internet Explorer and Firefox).

The Internet is an infinitely cool place, but so is that funky bar at Mos Eisley on Tatooine in the original *Star Wars* film (*Episode IV: A New Hope*). I think it would be great to actually visit such a place, but only if I came properly armed with a blaster or light saber. The Internet is exactly like that! There are wonderful, new and exciting things going on there—but you really shouldn't show up without knowing the risks, understanding how to defend yourself, and arming yourself with the right protection.

Chapter 2

Drive-By Malicious Code

Mom's Gonna Kill Me!

Meet Eric, from Novato, California, a normal teen who likes to create web pages for his friends. Eric spends a lot of time on the Internet. He is a major gamer, visits a lot of different sites looking for ideas, and likes to download free software.

Before Eric got his own laptop, he used his mom's computer to surf the Net and download free stuff. Eventually, Eric's mom's computer became so slow that it took *forever* to download software. That's when Eric asked a friend what to do. That's also when Eric found out that he should have had a firewall and downloaded patches to prevent hackers from getting in and planting spyware on his system. Eric thought that antivirus software was all he needed to protect him and he had never even heard of drive-by malicious code.

Eric found out the hard way that a hacker had back-doored his system and had been sifting confidential information from it. Well, not really Eric's system. It was his mom's system and her confidential information. Oops... sorry, Mom. Now, Eric has his own laptop with a firewall, current patches, antivirus software, and spyware protection.

So, what happened to Eric? He simply didn't have the right protection to keep the bad guys out and to keep the malicious code from getting in. Like most teens, he needed to know a lot more about security than he did. While virus protection is important, it's not the be-all and end-all of security. Malicious code can land on your system in *many* ways. You might simply have visited the wrong website and been hit by a drive-by. A *drive-by* is when you visit a website that has been outfitted to plant code onto your computer without your knowledge or consent.

Drive-by Download   Unwanted software that makes it onto your computer when you visit a website that has been outfitted to plant code onto your computer without your knowledge.

2.1 Why Does Malicious Code Exist?

When you consider the work that goes into writing software, you have to ask why anyone would care that much about trashing a stranger's computer system. Is it to prove that they can? Perhaps. To understand why people write malicious code, it helps to look first at WHO is doing the writing. We are starting to see a shift in computer crime as the motive for malicious code writers. However, many teens write malicious code for other reasons.

A surprising number of teens write malicious code. Teens figure prominently as both hackers and virus writers. (For reference, hackers and virus writers are NOT the same thing. This chapter talks about virus writers. To learn about hackers, read Chapter 4, "Spy vs. Spy.") A lot of research has gone into understanding why teenagers become virus writers. Some teens are interested for the sheer challenge of it. Others are motivated by different factors. Sarah Gordon, a security researcher, has done a lot of research in this area and points out that the most common feature among virus writers is that they don't really have a lot in common. Sarah's research finds that virus writers "vary in age, income level, location, social/peer interaction, educational level, likes, dislikes and manner of communication." While many teen virus writers write viruses for the sheer challenge of it others don't have the same ethical behavior and do not put those ethics into practice.

> *A surprising number of teens write malicious code.*

For some teens who write malicious code, there are heavy delusions of grandeur in the process. That was certainly the goal of Sven Jaschan, an 18-year-old German teen arrested in 2004 for creating Sasser.e, a variation on an earlier worm dubbed Netsky. Along with its predecessors, Sasser literally bombarded machines worldwide with millions of junk emails. As with many hackers, Jaschan's goal wasn't so much to disrupt Internet commerce as it was to make a name for himself. After his arrest, he told officials he'd only wanted to see his "creation" written about in all the world's papers. Jaschan told reporters, "It was just great how Netsky began to spread, and I was the hero of my class."

Is this admiration justified? Rarely. Consider the case of Jeffrey Lee Parson of Minnesota, another 18-year-old. Parson was arrested in 2003 for releasing a variant on the Blaster virus. While his friends and neighbors were taken in, at least briefly, the world of computing professionals was not. He used the Blaster code, created a variant, released it, and got caught. Not so bright after all.

Today, people still write viruses for the challenge or to become famous, but there are also those who write viruses to steal intellectual property from corporations, destroy corporate data, promote fraudulent activity, spy on other countries, create networks of compromised systems, and so on. And, those virus writers know that millions of computer systems are vulnerable, and they are determined to exploit those vulnerabilities. Does this mean that all the teens have turned into computer criminals? No. It simply means that with the widespread Internet, more people (including criminals) have access to it, and they are using it to commit crimes.

More information than ever is now stored on computers, and that information has a lot of value. You may not realize it, but your computer and your data are at higher risk than ever before. Even if your machine contains NO personal information, NO financial data, and nothing that could be of the slightest interest to anyone, your machine could still be used to attack someone else's. As Justin, a 16-year-old from Atherton, California said, "It's just not right that someone can take over my machine and use it." That's what can happen when your system is used to create a denial-of-service (DoS) attack. An attacker planted code on Justin's system without his knowledge and used his system to launch an attack against someone else. In a DoS attack, the victim is flooded with so much Internet traffic that legitimate users can't get through.

2.2 Viruses

A computer **virus** is a set of computer instructions that self-replicate. A virus can be a complete program (a file unto itself) or a piece of code—just part of a computer program file. In its most basic form, a virus makes copies of itself. MANY copies of itself, over and over again.

Some viruses also carry a payload. The payload tells the virus to do damage, such as delete files or attack other systems. I'll talk more about payloads in the next section.

Virus Number 1

Fred Cohen, then a doctoral student at the University of Southern California, wrote the first documented computer virus in 1983 as an experiment to study computer security. Officials were so concerned, they banned similar projects!

Even a virus without a payload can cause major problems. Just through the process of making copies of itself, even a simple virus can quickly use up all available memory in your computer. This can slow your computer down to a pathetic crawl, or even stop other programs from running altogether.

A computer virus is very much like a biological virus. The flu is a good example of a biological virus that can be transmitted from one person to another. Just how sick you get depends on the type of flu and whether you've been vaccinated. Once you're infected with the flu, you can also spread that virus to every person you come in contact with.

In the worst-case scenario, you could be another Typhoid Mary. As you probably know, Mary Mallon was an immigrant cook working in New York at the turn of the twentieth century. Apparently healthy herself, Mary spent much of her time between 1900 and 1915 spreading typhoid fever around town along with her signature peach desserts. Records tell us that she infected between 25 and 50 people and probably caused at least three deaths. After the third death, "Typhoid Mary" was placed in quarantine for the rest of her life. In the computer world, carriers have a much larger reach. While Typhoid Mary infected a mere 50 people during a span of 15 years, computer viruses and worms can infect thousands of other systems in just minutes. Consider the case of Code Red. When that worm was unleashed in 2001, it infected more than 250,000 systems in only nine hours. Many companies were hit hard because they weren't protected. In an ironic twist, one of the companies hit was actually Microsoft. The computer giant had neglected to apply its own patches to two of the servers used for its Hotmail web-based email service.

Virus   An independent program that makes copies of itself. LOTS of copies! A virus may sometimes also include a destructive payload-like code that deletes all your files.

Once a single computer is infected with a virus, it can infect hundreds of thousands of other computers. Just how much damage occurs depends on two things: (1) whether each computer in the chain is protected with current antivirus software, and (2) whether the virus carries a payload. If the virus carries a payload, it may perform harmful requests such as deleting all your data; if it does this, it can't continue to replicate because there are no programs for it to infect. Most viruses don't contain a payload; they simply replicate. That is, the average virus just copies itself from one computer to another. While this sounds harmless enough, the copying process uses up memory and disk space. This leaves affected computers running slowly, and sometimes not at all.

2.2.1 How Viruses Replicate

A virus is a self-replicating computer program. Its primary purpose is to make more and more copies of itself. Still, most viruses require human intervention to start replicating. For example, you may inadvertently trigger a virus to begin replicating when you click on an infected email attachment. Once a virus is activated, it can create and distribute copies of itself through email or other programs.

Here are some ways your machine can be infected by a virus:

- Sharing infected CDs
- Downloading and running infected software from the Internet
- Opening infected email attachments
- Visiting a malicious website

Just as the flu reappears each winter with just enough variations to negate last year's flu shot, once a virus is out there it can keep coming back again and again as new variants. Often, just a few simple tweaks to the code create a new variant of the virus. The more variants that are created, the more opportunities a virus can have to get access to your system. By mid-2005, Symantec AntiVirus was scanning for over 70,000 known threats.

When physicians check for a physical virus, they rely on a set of symptoms that together indicate the presence of that virus. Some antivirus programs use a signature to identify known viruses. You can think of the signature as a fingerprint. When crime scene investigators (CSIs) want to know whether a particular criminal has been on the scene, they check for that person's fingerprints. When antivirus software wants to know whether your machine has been infected with a particular virus, it looks for that virus' signature. Internally, the virus signature is a pattern of specific bits or bytes that will identify the virus. Keep in mind that *bit* is short for "binary digit." A bit is a single 0 or 1.

Signature A unique pattern of bits that antivirus software uses to identify a virus.

2.2.2 Malicious Payloads

All viruses are annoying. Some also have a destructive payload. A **payload** is a subset of instructions that deliberately do something nasty to your computer system—or someone else's. One of the earlier viruses, dubbed Happy99, used its payload simply to announce its presence. Any time you executed a program that had been infected with Happy99, the following message would display on your screen:

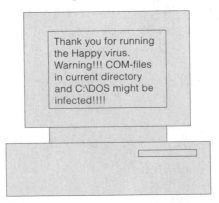

As a command file virus, Happy99 infected only command files (those files having a .COM file extension). Of course, at the time it was released users still relied on MS-DOS, so almost all important system operations (copying files, deleting files, even viewing a list of the files on your machine) still had to be done using MS-DOS command files—all of which had .COM file extensions.

Like Happy99, most early viruses attacked program and system files. A major change came in the 1990s, when virus writers stopped targeting programs and began to focus their efforts on documents. Unlike programs, which users rarely share indiscriminately, documents travel far and wide. During the writing of this book, the document that contains this chapter traveled between myself, my editor, a fact checker, the publisher, reviewers, and typesetting. Other documents are FAR more widely traveled. Job seekers may distribute hundreds of resumes via email or upload in search of that perfect position. The first virus to infect a Microsoft Word document was discovered in 1995, and it spread like wildfire. The Melissa virus, unleashed in 1999, gained international publicity and resulted in a jail sentence for its creator. When the user opened an infected file, the virus attempted to mail that file to up to 50 contacts defined in the user's Outlook Express address book.

Newer viruses include payloads that destroy or change your data, change your system settings, or send out your confidential information. The damage can be costly. When the Chernobyl virus payload was first triggered in 1999, nearly a million computers were affected in Korea alone, costing Korean users an estimated quarter of a **billion** dollars!

Where Do Viruses Come From?

Geographically, computer viruses are an awfully diverse lot. Some of the more well-known malicious code actually originated in some pretty unexpected places:

- Brain originated in Pakistan.
- Chernobyl, while referring to a Ukrainian city, originated in Taiwan.
- Michelangelo began in Sweden, not Italy.
- Tequila sounds Mexican, but originated in Switzerland.
- Yankee Doodle, surprisingly, really is an American virus!

A payload commonly used today initiates a denial-of-service (DoS) attack. This type of attack is usually aimed at a third-party website and attempts to prevent legitimate users from gaining access to that website by literally flooding the site with bogus connections from infected machines. Mydoom.F is a good example of a piece of malicious code with a destructive payload. Mydoom.F carries a payload that initiates a denial-of-service attack AND deletes picture files and documents on your PC.

2.2.3 Virus Hall of Shame

There are literally tens of thousands of computer viruses. Some are nasty; others funny. Still more are just annoying. Of the field, I found the viruses detailed in **Table 2.1** to be worthy of note.

Table 2.1 Famous Viruses

Virus Name	Release Date	Significance
Brain	1986	Brain was the first "stealth" virus that attempted to hide itself to avoid detection. One of the first viruses, Brain focused its attentions on low-density floppy disks back when the disks really were floppy (before widespread use of the smaller 3.5-inch disks since replaced by CDs). Brain didn't carry a payload but rendered disks unusable by copying itself into every free space so that disks that should have been empty or near empty registered as filled.
Stoned	1987	If political activism were a category of virus, Stoned would be its first member. Usually benign, this particular virus was more likely to annoy you than damage your data. What it was guaranteed to do was display the following message: "Your PC is now stoned! LEGALIZE MARIJUANA!"
Yankee Doodle	1989	Another cute virus brought to us by bored programmers. This one serenaded its victims by sending part of the tune *Yankee Doodle* to the system speakers every day at 5 p.m. Not to be satisfied with this musical extravaganza, later versions of this virus also searched for concurrent infestations of Ping Pong viruses and changed that malicious code to self-destruct after passing itself on 100 times. (One has to wonder whether the Yankee Doodle and Ping Pong virus writers were having some sort of competition.)

Virus Name	Release Date	Significance
Form	1990	Form was an example of just how badly a virus writer could program and still have an effective virus. Like most early viruses, Form ate up memory and played with disk space, but did neither in an especially effective way. It sometimes, but not always, displayed the following message: "The FORM-Virus sends greetings to everyone who's reading this text. FORM doesn't destroy data! Don't panic!" This was followed by an obscene message to someone named Corrine. On either the 18th or 24th of each month (depending on your source, or the variant of Form), this virus also caused strange clicking noises at each keystroke. While not intentionally damaging, the code was sloppy and contained bugs that could sometimes render floppy disks unusable and in rare cases completely kill the hard drive.

Tequila	1991	Strange as it sounds today, this was a virus that required considerable user input to function. Definitely the type of virus that could only work before home PC users were really aware of what viruses were and what they could do.
		
		When Tequila triggered, it displayed the following line:
		
		`Execute: mov ax, FE03 / int 21. Key to go on!.`
		
		If the user complied, Tequila then displayed this message:
		
		`Welcome to T. TEQUILA'S latest production`
		`Contact T. TEQUILAP/P.o. Box 543/6312 St'hausen/Switzerland`
		`Loving thoughts to L.I.N.D.A.`
		
		`BEER and TEQUILA forever !`
		
		Hardly inspiring for its intellectual prowess. Of more interest is that Tequila used a relatively new stealth technique, stealth-sizing. While earlier viruses hid their names from display (stealth-reading), Tequila also disguised the file size. (One of the ways you can tell that a file has been infected by a virus is that the file size jumps because of the added lines of code.)

Michelangelo	1991	This was the disaster that never happened. This virus was designed to delete user data on the trigger date, March 6—a date that also happened to be Michelangelo's birthday. Widely reported in the press, doomsayers prepped the world for up to 5 million affected machines. In the meantime, March 6 came and went and fewer than 10,000 incidents were reported worldwide. What Michelangelo actually accomplished was to make the average computer user aware of what a computer virus was and to spur massive sales of antivirus software.

continues

Table 2.1 Famous Viruses *(continued)*

Virus Name	Release Date	Significance
Cascade	Early 1990s	Another blast from the past, Cascade was one of the "cute" viruses intended to awe the afflicted. In this case, the virus caused displayed characters to "cascade" down the screen in waterfall style, landing in a big pile at the bottom of the screen. In an interesting twist, the writer intended this virus to afflict all machines except those made by IBM. Unfortunately for IBM users, his code didn't work as expected and those users were hit as well.
Concept	1995	Spread through Microsoft Word documents, this virus was one of the first to work on multiple operating systems (in this case, Windows 95 and Windows NT as well as most versions of Microsoft Word, including the Macintosh editions). Once a machine was infected, the virus compromised all Word documents created using the Save As command.
Laroux	1996	Another macro virus, this one afflicted Excel files. In its original form, this was a pure virus—existing only to duplicate itself and carrying no actual payload other than a text message that could only be seen by looking into the document code. But by 1999, Laroux had mutated. Newer versions usually just changed the Author, Subject, Title, and Keywords in the document properties to GTHOMSONZ. For files infected on the 16th or 30th of the month, however, Laroux also assigned a file password created at random. The data wasn't damaged per se, but it became awfully hard for the owner to get to.
Marburg	1998	An interesting virus, named after Marburg hemorrhagic fever, a nasty form of the Ebola virus that causes bleeding from the eyes and other body openings. The Marburg virus triggered three months (to the hour) after it infected a machine. When the user ran an infected program, Marburg displayed the Windows error icon randomly all over the computer screen. Random operating system errors followed. Probably more damaging than the virus payload itself was the fact that Marburg deleted the integrity databases of several antivirus products, putting the victim at risk from other viruses.
CH1	1998	Named for the Ukrainian nuclear reactor that imploded in 1986, this family of viruses actually originated in South-East Asia. As its name would imply, this was an especially nasty virus. When the virus triggered on the 26th of the month, it rendered the PC unable to boot AND overwrote the hard drive with garbage characters.

You'll note that many of these viruses are more historic than current. If you're wondering whether viruses are out of vogue, hardly! What's actually happened is that malicious code has advanced with technology. Old viruses evolved into new viruses (called *variants* or *mutations*), and new viruses are being created every day.

You'll also notice that much of the material in Table 2.1 is written in past tense. I talk about what these viruses did as if they no longer exist. That's not technically true. Viruses are a bit like socks that get lost in the washing machine. Somehow, they have a way of reappearing. So, most of the viruses listed in the table still exist in the wild corners of cyberspace. They're just no longer major threats. That's partly because some of these viruses target technology that's no longer in use. An even bigger factor, however, is that antivirus software now routinely searches for them. The truly dangerous viruses at any moment are the ones we don't yet know about; they have no names or descriptions.

2.2.4 Virus Writers

The nature of virus writers has evolved with the technology they exploit. The very first self-replicating programs existed mostly as technical exercises. For the most part, these were generated by graduate school programmers, often as research for doctoral theses. Early on, the field expanded to include teens looking for a technical challenge as well as the stereotypical loner geeks—socially awkward teens using malicious code to make names for themselves. These writers not only didn't hide their viruses very well, many didn't hide them at all. Their actual goal was to make as many people as possible aware of what they'd done.

Not surprisingly, many of these virus writers were caught and convicted of various computer crimes. They included Sven Jaschan, the German teenager who created Sasser, and Jeffrey Lee Parson, the Minnesota teen responsible for one of the many Blaster variants. Even today, nearly half of the viruses include "authorship" information. In some cases, those really are the names of the virus writers or the groups they represent. In other cases, named authors are themselves additional victims.

> **Wanted Dead or Alive!**
>
> Reminiscent of Old West bounties, a few malicious code victims have struck back by offering substantial rewards for the capture and conviction of worm and virus writers. Microsoft began the trend, offering $250,000 bounties, and then upping the ante to $500,000 on the Blaster and SoBig authors. Preparing for future attacks, on November 5, 2003 Microsoft funded the Anti-Virus Reward Program with $5 million in seed money to help law enforcement agencies round up malicious code writers. The SCO Group joined this effort in late January 2004, offering a $250,000 bounty on the MyDoom author.

More recently, however, professionals are joining the loop. Mikko Hypponen of the Finnish security firm F-Secure, notes, "We used to be fighting kids and teenagers writing viruses just for kicks…. Now most of the big outbreaks are professional operations." They're looking for cash, not infamy.

So where's the money enter in? In the case of adware worms and viruses, some worm writers actually receive royalties from the companies whose pop-up ads they enable. One such writer is Farid Essebar, known online as Diabl0. Diabl0 was responsible for the 2005 MyTob worm. One of the effects of MyTob was to lower security settings, enabling the display of pop-up ads that would otherwise have been blocked. Diabl0 claimed that he was paid by pop-up advertisers for every click-through (that is, every time a user clicked on such a pop-up). Many experts also believe that the MyDoom worm author was actually paid to create his program by spammers.

2.3 Worms

Often people refer to viruses and worms as the same things. However, there are two major distinctions between general viruses and worms: the ability to travel alone and the ability to stand alone as a separate program.

First, run-of-the-mill viruses require human intervention to start replicating. That is NOT true of worms. Worms can travel from one system to another across a network without any human intervention. A worm can make copies of itself on a network—for example, from one network disk drive to another—or move by itself using email or another transport mechanism.

Worm   A standalone malicious code program that copies itself across networks.

The second difference is that a worm is usually a standalone program. A worm program **transmits itself** between machines across a network. A general virus **attaches itself** to files. When a virus copies itself, it is copying itself to other files on the same machine. (A virus spreads to another machine when one of the infected files is moved to the other machine, in most cases by a user who does not realize that her files have been infected.) A worm copies itself to another machine rather than another file on the same machine.

The end result of all that copying is usually denied service. Someone, somewhere who actually wants to use a network resource can't get to it because the worm is taking up so much space or bandwidth. Often, worms initiate a denial-of-service (DoS) attack against a specific website. Code Red targeted the White House website; Blaster targeted Microsoft's update site. In the case of Code Red, sheer luck (and very fast counter-programming) prevented the worm from fulfilling the FBI's assessment of its danger—the possibility of bringing down the entire Internet! Officials feared that the worm would use up so many network resources that the entire Internet would become impossible for legitimate users to use.

Other worms send out so much garbage data that substantial parts of the Internet itself stop responding. Financially, this can be devastating. When Slammer brought the Net to its knees in 2003, Continental Airlines had to cancel flights from Newark, New Jersey, because it couldn't process tickets. Even more frightening is that Slammer brought down emergency services. Outside Seattle, 911 dispatchers lost access to their call centers. While no deaths were directly reported from this outage, fate could easily have taken another turn.

> **Worm Number 1**
>
> In the early 1980s, Xerox researchers John Shoch and Jon Hupp designed an application to automate installing and updating software across a network. When that application hit a bug, it distributed the bug as well. Shoch and Hupp noted, "The embarrassing results were left for all to see: 100 dead machines scattered about the building." They had unwittingly created the first network worm.

Our society relies on computer networks for a lot more than just banking and education. The 2004 outbreak of Sasser was widely believed to have crashed a train radio network, leaving 300,000 train travelers stranded in Sydney, Australia. Of course, computer networks link more than just our transportation systems. They also link our hospitals and ambulances. Many traffic lights are also computer-controlled. It may only be a matter of time until those "cute" pranks prove deadly.

Worms have many ways of getting into your system without your knowledge. For example, they can make their way into your computer from the Internet through a security flaw. You might run a cool game on your computer, but it is really a worm that tricked you into running it by making you think it was only a game.

Sometimes, you don't need to do anything. Some of the more devastating worms, such as Code Red and Slammer, actually spread with NO action required by the user at all.

Unlike most viruses, most worms are designed to be *fast*. The speed at which they are released once a security flaw is found but before a patch is released is amazingly fast. It used to take six months before you would see attacks hit the Net. Today, it's six days.

The 2003 infestation of the worm Blaster (also known as MSBlast and Lovesan) demonstrated how fast these worms are released and the speed with which a worm can spread throughout the Internet. Blaster razed networks just *27 days* after the vulnerability was publicly disclosed. To make matters worse, script kiddies started to release variants.

Script Kiddie   A low-talent hacker who uses easy, well-known techniques to exploit Internet security vulnerabilities. A script kiddie typically takes code already written by the true expert, uses it and sometimes modifies it. In the hacker community, being called a script kiddie is a major insult.

One infamous script kiddie was Jeffrey Lee Parson. While still in high school, he released a variant on the Blaster worm. The real malicious code writer—the person who wrote the original Blaster worm—was never found. Parson was just a copycat. Like Parson, almost anyone can make minor alterations to code. It doesn't require the same depth of skill or creativity that you would need to actually create a worm or virus. Still, the effects of minor alterations can be devastating. Mere weeks after Parson unleashed his Blaster variant, experts estimated that the worm had infected 500,000 computers worldwide. Even that wasn't all his own work. Parson's Blaster variant only infested 7,000 computers. After that, variants on his variant created by still other virus writers took over.

As worms continue to become more complex and evolved, it isn't just the rate of variant creation that's speeding up. Infection speeds have also dramatically increased. During the Code Red worm attack in 2001, the number of machines infected doubled every 37 minutes. At the peak of the Slammer worm attack in 2003, the number of machines infected doubled every 8.5 seconds!

2.3.1 Especially Wicked Worms

Like viruses, worms exist in many shapes and forms. **Table 2.2** details some of the more notable worms.

Table 2.2 Famous Worms

Worm Name	Release Date	Significance
Morris worm	1988	Robert Morris, Jr., a Cornell graduate student, was responsible for what is generally considered to be the first worm released to the Internet. This worm affected 6,000 to 9,000 major Unix machines, collected passwords along the way, and shut down a good bit of the Internet as it existed at that time. Morris himself became the first worm writer arrested for his exploits. (He served three years probation, performed 400 hours of community service, and was fined $10,000 plus costs.)
Melissa	1999	Melissa was a blended threat that included a virus that attacked Microsoft Word documents. When users opened an infected document, Melissa accessed the user's email address book and mailed itself to up to 50 people.
I Love You	2000	The I Love You worm hit computers worldwide in May 2000, arriving in the form of emails having the Subject line "I love you" and carrying the attachment Love-Letter-For-You.txt.vbs. Readers who opened that attachment had their PCs searched for passwords, which were emailed back to a website in the Philippines. The worm then re-sent itself to every contact in the reader's Outlook Express address book. This worm makes the list for using social engineering to create a message that even readers who knew better simply HAD to read. (My editor personally knew a systems manager in a computer firm who had to sheepishly explain to her manager why on earth she thought a sales representative would send her a love letter....)
Code Red	2001	Code Red attacked websites rather than PCs. First, Code Red defaced infected sites with the following message: Hello! Welcome to http://www.worm.com! Hacked By Chinese! At the trigger time, midnight July 19th, infected servers then stopped infecting other servers and initiated a massive coordinated DoS attack against the official White House website. This attack failed only because experts identified the target—on the 18th, less than 24 hours in advance—and moved the White House website to a different Internet address. Code Red set speed records, both in its spread and in the rate at which mutations occurred. An especially nasty mutation appeared during the first infestation of this worm. That mutation pushed infection rates to a peak of 2,000 servers per minute!

continues

Table 2.2 Famous Worms (continued)

Worm Name	Release Date	Significance
Nimda	2001	Nimda was a much more complex worm than its predecessors, on several levels. First, Nimda actually used four methods to pass itself on. Once a machine was infected, Nimda infected executable files (such as games), mailed itself to every email address available, spread itself across any connected local area network, and finally searched out Internet websites to attack remotely from the infected machine.
		Nimda was also especially scary because users could be infected simply by clicking on the subject line of an infected email message; they didn't need to actually read the message or execute an attachment. Nimda could also spread to users who simply visited infected websites.
		Nimda worked with backdoors on several levels as well. First, Nimda made use of trapdoors left by earlier worms, including variants of Code Red. Nimda then left its own backdoor, allowing malicious hackers full access to infected machines.
Blaster	2003	Also known as the Lovesan worm. This worm targeted Microsoft, initiating a DoS attack against http://windowsupdate.com/.
Slammer	2003	Also known as Sapphire, and "the worm that crashed the Internet in 15 minutes," Slammer wins the award for fastest Internet worm. When it hit in January 2003, Slammer literally slammed into the Internet at full speed. Within 10 minutes, Slammer had infected 90% of its targets. Within 15 minutes, important parts of the Internet became unusable.
Welchia	2003	Also called Nacho, Welchia was a rather interesting variation, a worm-killing worm. Welchia's main task (other than spreading itself), appeared to be deleting infestations of the Blaster worm and applying the Microsoft patch to prevent similar attacks. While the intentions were good, the results weren't always pleasant. Applying updates requires expert supervision to avoid causing one problem while fixing another. Many machines crashed from the unsupervised updates.
Netsky	2004	Another mass-mailing worm, Netsky used social engineering to trick users, arriving as emails that purported to be valid delivery notification messages. Part of a fairly strange "worm war," some variants of Netsky actually attacked and removed parts of other worms (usually, Bagel and MyDoom).
Sasser	2004	Like Blaster, and unlike so many other worms, Sasser was NOT a mass-mailer. Instead, it attacked via operating system security holes and spread without user intervention.

Worm Name	Release Date	Significance
MyDoom	2004	In a unique twist, MyDoom appeared to have been commissioned by spammers to allow sending of spam (unsolicited advertisement) email from compromised computers. Actually a blended threat, MyDoom used both email and network pathways to spread. The email attack was especially widespread. MyDoom not only emailed everyone you did know, it also randomly generated email addresses, hitting people who weren't in your address book as well. Using spoofed subject lines, MyDoom emails relied on social engineering, getting victims to open emails that appeared to be from people they knew. Roughly a quarter of the infected machines also launched a DoS attack against the software firm SCO Group.

2.3.2 Variants and Mutations

With a biological virus, a single tiny mutation in the virus can mean that the vaccine no longer works. With a computer virus, a tiny variation in the code can prevent antivirus software from identifying the virus. Virus writers know that once someone creates a new virus, they can simply add a few tweaks and get their variant of that virus past the antivirus engine.

Some viruses are polymorphic and can alter themselves. That is, to hide from detection, polymorphic viruses change their signatures every time they replicate and infect a new file. Fortunately, antivirus software can

Got a Minute?

At top speed, Code Red infected over 2,000 servers a minute!

detect many new variants through the use of heuristics. Antivirus programs detect viruses by analyzing the program's structure, behavior, and other attributes, rather than looking for a signature. Still, variants and mutations continue to cause problems as no publicly available antivirus product can detect every virus in the world.

While a single worm or virus is bad enough, few pieces of malicious code remain in their initial states for long. The original authors, as well as other malicious code writers, continuously produce new variations on old attacks. Code Red is a good example. This worm actually mutated during its initial release. Of course, Code Red is hardly the only one. The MyTob worm, introduced in early March 2005, had given rise to 12 additional mutations by month end. Netsky inspired even more mutations. While released in early 2004, by mid-year Netsky had evolved into 29 variants. By June 2004, there were also 10 variants on MyDoom and 28 variants of Bagel!

This is why your antivirus software must be up to date. If your virus software hasn't been updated since last week, you don't have the new signatures. And last week's signatures might identify last week's viruses, but not this week's new viruses and mutations. Most mutations are changed just enough to render the last virus signature invalid. To avoid getting slammed by last week's news, always make sure your antivirus software is configured to download updates *automatically* from your antivirus vendor. Don't forget antivirus software is only one piece of the security puzzle. Firewalls and intrusion detection/prevention systems can also detect/prevent various worms and can be used to prevent unwanted connections (see "Firewalls" in Chapter 11, "Any Port in a Storm."). Intrusion detection software is often bundled into firewall software—software that allows you to detect and sometimes block known attacks from getting into your network.

Variant   A mutated form of a virus or worm. Variants are usually just different enough that the original virus signature won't match.

2.4 Trojan Horses

A Trojan horse (sometimes simply called a Trojan) is a piece of software that appears to be a legitimate software application or game. It might masquerade as a free version of a popular game, or be hidden in a commercial game. In August 1998, MGM Interactive announced apologetically that the master CD of its popular *Wargames* was infected with the Marburg virus. It had become an unwitting Trojan.

The idea with any Trojan is that it needs to be enticing enough that users will want to run it. In reality, the real purpose of many Trojans is to open a backdoor to your computer that allows for easy reentry. A backdoor is an easy entry point into a system that the unsuspecting user does not know exists. This allows the virus writer to return later and steal your confidential information or even use your machine to attack someone else's. This backdoor to your computer allows someone else to control your computer system or access your files without your permission or knowledge.

Sometimes, running a Trojan can unleash a computer virus or a worm. This combination of nasty code operating together is called a blended threat. By attacking in several ways simultaneously, blended threats can spread rapidly and cause widespread damage.

Blended Threat   A form of malicious code that includes more than just one attack. A blended threat could include a virus, a worm, a Trojan horse, and a DoS attack all in one attack.

The name "Trojan horse" derives from Greek mythology. In an exploit reported by the epic poet Virgil in the *Aeneid*, the Greeks gained entrance to the city of Troy by presenting the Trojans with a gift of a giant wooden horse. Delighted by the gift, the Trojans took the horse beyond the gates and into the city. Overnight, scores of Greek soldiers who had hidden inside the Trojan horse emerged. They slew the Trojans in their sleep and opened the gates of their city.

In computer terms, a Trojan horse has a similar objective: to camouflage itself as something harmless or desirable, then to open the door and let attackers in. Just as the ancients learned to "Beware of Greeks bearing gifts," you should always question the motives and real purposes behind free software.

Also be aware that you can run a Trojan program without actually knowing that you are doing so. One of the more annoying Trojans making the rounds in recent years has been Vundo (also known as Adware.VirtuMonde). Part of an adware program, the Vundo Trojan downloads and displays pop-up ads. The Trojan itself is downloaded to your machine when you click the link for a specific website sent out in spammed email. At no point do you actually need to run the program; many users never even realize they've been infected. They simply notice a higher number of pop-ups. Also, not all pop-ups originate locally from adware/spyware—many pop-up advertisements originate from websites themselves.

You can run a Trojan program without actually knowing that you are doing so.

While pop-up ads are certainly annoying, other Trojans are far more damaging. For example, the I Love You virus planted a Trojan that recorded user passwords and emailed those passwords back to the virus writer.

That particular Trojan also overwrote picture files (.jpg files) with copies of the I Love You virus. The Worm.ExploreZip Trojan searches the user's hard drives and destroys PowerPoint, Excel, and Word documents as well as additional files. Other Trojans install backdoors and even keyboard loggers—silently capturing passwords and personal data as the user types unaware.

2.5 Bot Networks

The Zombie Machine

One fine day in March 2004, Tabitha, a junior at Gettysburg Area High School, got off the school bus and ran home to check her email. Because she has friends (both real and virtual) spread around much of the world, this is something she does at least three times a day. No Internet. Three hours later, still no Internet. And, no Internet still later that evening.

Assuming there was a problem with her service, Tabitha had her father brave the rounds of "Please hold" and recorded ads to actually talk to her cable company. What they learned was unexpected and pretty frightening. Earlier that day, her cable company had tracked hundreds of attacks coming from her connection. Seeing the massive outflow of email, the cable company cut off her service. Unfortunately, they didn't tell her.

Tabitha was clueless. Like a growing number of home users, Tabitha's parents had networked their home. A simple router split her Internet cable, allowing access from both her computer and her parent's machine. Apparently, her computer had been the victim of a Bot network attack that got past the router firewall. Someone else had taken control and was using her PC to launch attacks against other computers. The attacker had literally turned her computer into a "zombie" machine.

This teenager's computer had become part of a bot network. A **bot** network is a collection of compromised machines often called **zombies**. Each zombie machine is under the command and control of the virus writer or hacker—almost always without the knowledge of the machine's rightful owner. The owner of the botnet can issue instructions from a central location, and all the zombies will carry out these instructions, often to attack more hosts. Tabitha certainly had no idea that her PC had been enlisted in a bot army. Likewise, Tabitha had no idea who took over her machine. She didn't even know what website they were trying to attack. If her father hadn't called the cable company, she may never have even known that her PC had been hijacked. What she did know was that losing her own service, however temporarily, was incredibly frustrating. She also found the idea of having some stranger control her computer just plain creepy.

Zombie or Bot   A computer that has been compromised by a piece of code that allows it to be controlled remotely without the computer owner's knowledge.

Usually, a **bot network** is a network of computers that have been unknowingly infected with a worm or Trojan, which installs code known as a bot that allows the attacker to launch remote commands and use the systems for future attacks. Basically, the bot opens a backdoor that allows the hacker to control the machine and initiate commands remotely.

Bot Network   A collection of remotely controlled infected machines. Hackers often use bot networks to launch attacks against corporate websites, or individuals as a result of an online dispute in a gaming or social network.

Once a hacker has assembled a bunch of machines compromised with bots, what he has is literally an army of bots that can be used to attack other machines, usually by flooding the target with connection requests, or data packets.

Basically, the bots execute a denial-of-service (DoS) attack where so many compromised machines try to connect to a single website that the site itself crashes. In this type of attack, the goal is to flood the target machine with data packets. The data transmitted is usually harmless itself, but the large amount of traffic consumes the target machine's bandwidth. It uses up the Internet resources available to the target machine, keeping it from being able to communicate properly.

The end result is the same in all cases. Legitimate users are denied service because of all the bogus traffic.

DoS   A denial-of-service attack. In a DoS attack, the victim is flooded with so much Internet traffic that legitimate users can't get through.

In recent years, bot networks have been used to attack some of the biggest names in the computing and corporate worlds. Microsoft, Amazon, Yahoo! and even CNN.com have been on the receiving ends of DoS attacks by bot networks. Because bot networks are assembled randomly across the World Wide Web, a single command can launch a DoS attack by bot networks at any time, from any place in the world. Indeed, the majority of machines compromised by bots are outside the United States.[1] To keep bots off your system, make sure you fill your Internet security shopping list (antivirus, spyware protection, PC software firewall, router with firewall, and patches) before you surf the Net.

If the threats have been growing, so have the attacks. In a single attack in June of 2004, a massive bot army of compromised home PCs managed to virtually shut down the websites of Apple Computer, Google, Microsoft, and Yahoo! for a full 2 hours. How could a single attack kill the websites of four major computer firms at one time? In this case, by focusing on a fifth computer firm, Akamai. Akamai runs domain name servers that translate domain names, such as www.microsoft.com, into the numerical addresses used by the Internet. Basically, Akamai controls the address book that takes Internet users to certain websites. It so happened that Apple Computer, Google, Microsoft, and Yahoo! were all Akamai clients.

So what can you do to keep your machine from attacking Microsoft? It would seem that the logical solution is to patch your machine. You need to make sure that you've applied all the current patches to your operating system and web browser (for patching, go to Chapter 14, "Tweaks"). However, the real question is how to protect yourself from bad bots (i.e., zombie makers). The first step, as in almost all computer security issues, is to make sure your antivirus software is installed correctly and ALWAYS up to date. It must include anti-spyware and anti-adware detection and removal capabilities. And you should make sure your PC is sitting behind a very well-defined firewall. For details, you can read about firewalls in Chapter 11.

---

1. For the first half of 2004, Symantec reported that the country with the largest percentage of known bots (25.2%) was the United Kingdom. Experts believe this is because the UK has one of the largest distributions of broadband service, and many of those home users never installed security.

2.6 Avoiding Malicious Code

Avoiding malicious code is getting to be a lot more complicated than it used to be. In the past, users could protect themselves fairly well simply by not sharing documents and not opening email attachments from people they didn't know. Today, that's just not enough. Today's user needs to know what to do as well as what not to do. He or she also needs a general understanding of social engineering.

2.6.1 What to Do (and What NOT to Do)

The first step to protecting yourself from nasty code is to be proactive as well as reactive. Make sure you have the basics covered:

- Install a top-rated antivirus package.

- Download software only from known websites. You also need to beware of malicious code masquerading as freeware. The Skulls.L Trojan, which affects certain types of cell phones, was actually advertised for free download using the name of a legitimate antivirus package from F-Secure. Victims thought they were downloading a free version of antivirus software when they were actually downloading a new virus! If you do download free software, make sure you do so from the manufacturer's website and not a third party.

- Use the automatic update option on your antivirus software. Remember that new mutations appear continuously. Automatic updates will help to keep your virus signatures current.

- Be wary of email from people you don't know. Of course, NEVER open attachments to emails of unknown origin.

- Also be wary of email from people you do know. Many worms re-send themselves to every person in a victim's online address book. Think long and hard before opening an attachment that you weren't expecting. If you were not expecting the attachment, call the sender before you open it, and ask that person if he or she sent it.

2.6.2 Understanding Social Engineering

Nasty code has been around for over 20 years now. We all know that opening attachments is dangerous, and sharing files can leave you without valid files of your own. Still, every year millions of users fall victim. Why?

A common theme is the use of **social engineering**. Social engineering involves understanding human nature and using that understanding to take advantage of users. It allows malicious code writers to trick users into breaking their own security rules. Sarah Granger, writing for SecurityFocus, put it well when she defined social engineering as "a hacker's clever manipulation of the natural human tendency to trust."

A good example of the use of social engineering to spread malicious code was seen in the May 2000 Love Bug attack. Most people who opened this virus did so for one of three reasons—all related to basic human psychology:

- The email came from someone they knew and trusted—a colleague, a spouse, an old friend. Someone who might possibly really love them.

- They thought the email was a joke. Millions of jokes (some much worse than others) circulate the Internet each day. For home users, these humorous anecdotes account for a good percentage of email usage.

- They just couldn't help themselves. "I love you" messages from distant colleagues, regardless of how unlikely and bizarre, simply jolt the recipient's curiosity.

Social engineering   Using general knowledge of human behavior to trick users into breaking their own security rules.

Of course, social engineering touches more than users' romantic lives. Some common uses of social engineering in malicious code include guessing passwords, spoofing emails to appear to come from acquaintances, masquerading as authority figures, warning about virus infestations, and never underestimating the human capacity for greed.

Password Guessing

The best passwords involve numbers and letters strung together in meaningless ways. We also all know that no one can ever remember those types of passwords. So, most people ignore password rules whenever possible and choose words and phrases they find easy to remember. English words as well as spouse's and children's names all appear frequently as passwords. A casual survey of British office workers conducted for the InfoSecurity Europe 2003 conference found that 12% actually used the word *password* as their password. Also, 16% used their own name, and 11% used the name of their favorite soccer team.

Where sites reject words that appear in English dictionaries, bilingual Americans often substitute common Spanish words. When sites require them to use numbers, most users select phone numbers, birthdates, or social security numbers. Again, all easy numbers for hackers to guess using readily available password "crackers." Compounding the problem, many users set the same username and password for all accounts, allowing hackers to have a field day with a single harvested password.

Don't I Know You?

People love keeping in touch with their pasts. Spammers rely on this, often generating Subject lines that trick users into believing that they might know the message sender. The Love Bug virus relied heavily on this factor to entice users to open the attachment.

You've Got a Virus! Fix It Now!

The Skulls.L Trojan discussed earlier is one of a growing number of attacks that masquerade as antivirus software. An early variation on this began appearing on chat networks and IM in 2002. Users received a message along the lines of the following:

You are infected with a virus that lets hackers get into your machine and read ur files, etc. I suggest you to download *[malicious url]* and clean ur infected machine. Otherwise you will be banned from *[IRC network]*.

Despite the awkward phrasing and "badly grammared" English, surprising numbers of users did just that, thus infecting their machines with Trojans that then initiated DoS attacks against other sites. According to the CERT Coordination Center at Carnegie Mellon, tens of thousands of machines were affected. (The CERT Coordination Center serves as a central command post for passing information during security emergencies, such as Code Red, and for collecting information to help prevent security breaches.)

Whatchya Got for Me?

As the number of "freebie" sites online attests to, computer users find freebies hard to turn down. Not surprisingly, many Trojans are embedded in free music downloads and free software. Countless lines of personal data are also harvested for future use via pop-ups informing users of free trips, valuable prizes, and hard cash they have "won."

Chapter 3

Data Grabbers and Dumpers

What? No Free Lunches?!

Meet Stef from Camden, Maine. Stef loves music and enjoys download-ing the latest hits to her iPod.

When Stef received an email offering her 10 free songs, she didn't hesi-tate to click the embedded link for more details. Now her PC is under siege from advertisers and continually plagued with pop-up ads.

Stef thought she was only getting a few songs. Little did she know that "free" on the Internet doesn't always mean free.

Stef thought her antivirus software protected her from having adware dumped on her system. She's not the only one. People think of adware and spyware as malicious code, but they are really in a category of their own. McAfee refers to them as **potentially unwanted programs**, or **PUPs**. That's a bit generous, since most spyware is unwanted, and I've yet to meet anyone who *really* wanted adware either.

Still, those PUPs are being dumped on systems all the time. This software includes adware, spyware, hijackers, cookies, and keyboard loggers. These are all **data grabbers**—programs that collect information about you (often without your knowledge) and send that information on to someone else or save it in a special file for pickup at the convenience of the hacker. Sometimes, that third party uses the information to target advertising. They're basically looking for better ways to sell you things. Other times, that information is used to steal your identity or take over your computer.

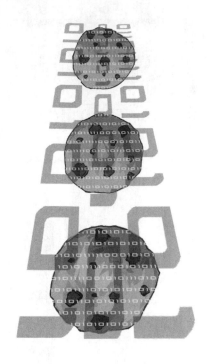

PUPs *(Potentially Unwanted Programs)*   A politically correct term for unwanted adware and spyware.

To find out just how much unwanted software was being dumped, the people at Symantec (who make Norton AntiVirus) decided to run a test in 2005. They took a brand-new computer, just out of the box, and hit the Net. What's important here is what they didn't do in advance. They didn't install antivirus or anti-adware software. They also didn't apply outstanding security patches to the operating system or web browser. What they found was astounding. After a single hour of surfing the Net, they examined the machine for unwanted software. The results were frightening. After the researchers surfed children's websites, they found 259 pieces of unwanted adware! And all the sites left enough cookies to open a bakery. (Cookies track the websites you've visited.) **Table 3.1** provides the breakdown.

Table 3.1 Symantec's "Unwanted Software" Study

Site Category	Adware	Spyware	Hijackers	Cookies
Sports	17	2	0	72
Kids	259	0	3	31
Gaming	23	4	2	68
News	3	1	0	26
Reseller	2	1	1	22
Shopping	0	0	0	0
Travel	64	2	1	35

Data grabbers   Software programs that collect information about you and send that data on to a third party. Data grabbers include adware, spyware, and keyboard loggers.

3.1 Spyware

Spyware is a relatively new form of malicious code. Some companies sell legitimate spyware programs. In this book, however, I cover malicious spyware. That is, an illegal program installed without your knowledge that can eat up system resources, affect performance, and steal confidential information. As the name suggests, spyware literally spies on you when you use your computer. Among other things, it may keep track of which websites you visit and what you do on those sites. In some cases, the spyware may also include keyboard-logging features that collect the user names and passwords you enter at various sites. Depending on the spyware author's motives, the end goal may be to steal your personal information or even your identity.

Spyware   A software program that monitors your computer usage without your knowledge. Spyware keeps track of which websites you visit and what you do on those sites. Put simply, it spies on you.

Spyware is different from the worms and viruses I talked about in the last chapter in that spyware's primary purpose is to spy on you. It doesn't self-replicate. Even so, spyware is just as dangerous to computer users as viruses and worms. In fact, spyware is more likely to leave your machine unusable (by eating up your bandwidth) than many viruses. Dell Computers reports that while spyware problems accounted for 4% of customer service calls in 2003, that number quadrupled in early 2004. By October 2004, around one in every four to five calls to Dell's support lines were related to spyware problems.

In a cruel twist, some spyware exists only to sell anti-spyware solutions. In October 2004, the Federal Trade Commission filed charges against three companies, Seismic Entertainment Productions, Smartbot.Net, and Sanford Wallace, for what amounted to spyware extortion. The three firms first infected PCs with spyware that overwhelmed users with unwanted pop-up ads, and then tried to sell them anti-spyware programs to fix the problems they'd just caused.

Unfortunately, there are also plenty of other types of spyware. There is also **adware**, a product very similar to spyware, which tracks your online activities to sell to advertisers.

If you care about a fast connection, online gaming, and privacy, you need to know the risks associated with unwanted spyware programs that install without your knowledge. You need to understand how spyware lands on your machine and whether you or your parents are at risk.

If your system has slowed down for no apparent reason, you may already have spyware on your system because you simply visited the wrong website and the program installed without your knowledge. This type of code dumping is called a **drive-by download**. Some spyware will even install after you say no to installing it.

Drive-by download   A program that is installed without your knowledge when you visit a compromised website, or a website specifically designed to download data grabbers.

3.2 Adware

Depending on whom you ask, either **adware** is a legal commercial software or it was dumped on the system without the user's knowledge. Some people refer to adware and spyware as the same thing, but they're not.

Adware is a type of software that delivers targeted advertising to your web browser. Adware does this by tracking what you do on the Web, which is why it's often confused with spyware. Advertisers use this tracking for what they call "behavioral targeting." It allows them to target ads to the consumers most likely to purchase a given product based on those consumers' other online activities. Adware giant Claria claims that "the relevancy of the messages drives click-through and conversion rates up to 40 times higher than traditional banner ads." For advertisers, this is a bonanza. There actually are some legitimate uses for adware, and most adware manufacturers try to stay within the letter of the law by requiring users to consent to having their programs installed.

Adware   A program that tracks user activities online and uses that tracking information to deliver Internet ads specifically targeted to each user.

At its worst, adware can be incredibly annoying, because it fills your screen with pop-up ads, it often slows down your computer, and it can be installed without your knowledge. Adware can change your homepage, flood you with multiple pop-up ads, install toolbars in your web browser, and read cookies installed on your computer. Sometimes, however, a user agrees to accept some adware as a condition of use for other free software, such as popular file-sharing programs.

Teens who are heavy Internet users can easily get adware dumped on their PCs without realizing it. These programs can hitch a ride when you download free tools such as screensavers. Teens often download adware along with popular software, music, and video files.

How Broad Is Broadband?

The spread of adware and spyware has been spurred by massive increases in the number of broadband Internet users. How massive?

By 2004, 37.9 million Americans had high-speed Internet connections. Even more telling, broadband services were available to nearly 99% of Americans.

Thanks to adware, the Internet is becoming nearly as ad infested as prime time TV. While adware is often unwanted software, sometimes it's more of an "I'll scratch your back if you scratch mine" situation. In a common scenario, many websites will allow you to download "free" software in exchange for taking adware as part of the package. Of course, that software really isn't free. You're *selling your time* in watching all the pop-ups in exchange for the software. This may not necessarily be a bad deal. Consider: If your cable company gave you free cable TV in exchange for using a system that stopped you from filtering out the commercials, you might still feel you were getting the better end of the bargain. That's pretty much the deal you're making when you use some popular file-sharing software, such as Kazaa. The trick is to realize the deal you're making.

3.2.1 End User Licensing Agreement (EULA)

Often, you may not realize the deal you're making—that is, many users don't realize that they've consented to install adware because they don't read the End User Licensing Agreement (EULA) when they install new software or sign up for new Internet services. This is understandable. EULAs can be, and typically are, long and boring, like a very long legal contract. Often, they're presented in small type and confusing language, and most users wrongly assume they don't cover anything that's terribly important.

EULA (End User Licensing Agreement) This is the detailed legalese document that you must agree to in order to install most programs.

Some EULAs have adware functions listed in the agreement. This type of download leaves the adware company on legal ground, because they can argue that you said yes to installing it in the first place, even though you may feel you were tricked. What a nice place to put an agreement like this—hidden in a EULA (pronounced YOO-la) that no one reads in the first place! This might prompt you to read EULAs carefully and completely before agreeing to the terms.

3.2.2 Peer-to-Peer (P2P) Networks

Email is not the only place to distribute malicious code. As the use of file sharing and peer-to-peer (P2P) networking increases, P2P sites become a great place to spread malicious code. Because P2P sites often have little or no security in place, they provide a rather fast car on the Internet freeway for virus writers to drive malicious code into your home.

P2P security issues are especially important for teens because teens tend to download stuff from everywhere on the Internet. That's a habit that can get you into a lot of trouble. Downloading software from reputable sites is a lot less risky, because these sites tend to be extremely careful about the software they allow to be downloaded. Things get riskier when you start downloading from unknown sites and sites that rely on individual submissions such as P2P networks. Downloading games, movies, and music from unknown sites can get you into trouble on several levels: malicious code, adware, spyware, Trojans, and keyboard loggers, not to mention the legal issues.

You Downloaded WHAT?!!!!

"Free" software is a common source of Trojans, so be extremely careful about what you download. It's especially risky to download free games and pirated software or movies. Think about it. If your goal is to download stolen goods (yes, that is what pirated software is!), how surprised should you really be that your source isn't trustworthy?

Even when you're downloading items from a legitimate source, make sure your virus checker is always running and up to date. Also, be especially careful of anything that was just posted. You might be downloading a brand-new virus for which a signature does not exist yet. Wait at least a few days and let someone else test the new goods for safety!

Giving Away Your Right to Privacy

Even if the material you're downloading is safe, your download experience may be more than you expected. Specifically, you may have agreed to accept adware when you installed the software you need for P2P file sharing.

Many teens use P2P file-sharing software to download music, movies, and games. Kazaa is an especially popular package. While Kazaa may not be specifically targeted at teens, they're obviously expecting heavy usage by minors. Embedded within the Kazaa EULA, several screens down (past the place where most users give up reading), you'll find the following notice:

9.4 Embedded Third Party Software

9.4.1 Cydoor. The software application you are about to install is supported by advertising revenue, meaning that we display ads as an integral part of our interface. This allows us to provide you with our software for free: the advertising income we receive supports for our development and distribution efforts.

We have partnered with Cydoor Technologies Ltd. ("Cydoor") to deliver advertisements to the application interface and computer, such as banner ads, buttons, or other advertising formats when you are using the software application. Cydoor's ad-serving technology allows us to display rotating advertisements on our application and to generate income from these advertisements. Our partnership with Cydoor enables us to avoid charging you for the software. ...

At this point you're probably thinking, but I really *need* to download free stuff! That's one of the reasons I wanted a PC to begin with. Don't despair. While you may or may not *need* to download programs, you certainly don't *need* to use an adware version of download software to do so. Many P2P services offer a commercial download package that's free of adware. The catch, of course, is that it is commercial, meaning you'll need to pay for it. In the case of Kazaa, the ad-free version, Kazaa Plus, sells for $29.95. If the price tag makes you balk, remember that you ARE paying for the free downloads. You're *selling your time* (to watch ads) and *details on your personal browsing habits*. For many people, that price is simply too high. The choice is yours to make.

3.3 Keyboard Loggers

Some keyboard loggers are integral parts of certain adware and spyware programs. Other keyboard loggers are installed separately as standalone programs, and marketed as forensic or monitoring systems.

A **keyboard logger** is exactly what it sounds like, a program that logs every keystroke that you type at your computer. This can be incredibly dangerous. Just think about some of the things that you type in. If you use online banking, you enter the user name and password for your bank account, maybe even the account number. If you order games or clothes online, you enter your parents' credit card number. If you apply for credit or jobs online, you enter your social security number and other personal data—everything a thief would need to take over your identity.

Keyboard Logger   A program that keeps track of every keystroke that you type at your computer.

Hackers have been planting keyboard loggers on users' PCs without their knowledge for many years. Sometimes, users even choose to load keyboard-logging programs. One such program is Gator eWallet. This program helps you to fill in online forms by remembering the information you most commonly need: name, address, user names, passwords, credit card numbers, etc. According to the publisher, adware giant Claria, only the user's first name, ZIP Code, and country are harvested. Still, there is a price for the convenience of having forms filled out automatically. When you agree to download eWallet, you are also agreeing to download Offer-Companion, a program that displays pop-up ads when you visit specific websites. You agree to this when you accept the EULA in downloading.

At least with eWallet, you know that you're installing a keyboard logger, and your financial data is protected. That isn't always the case. In recent years, it's become increasingly easy for third parties to plant these logging devices remotely without your knowledge.

Short of outlawing keyboard loggers, which probably wouldn't help anyway, the only solution to this problem is to adequately protect your machine against drive-by downloads. Outlawing loggers isn't an option anyway. Keyboard loggers are a standard part of any security expert's tool bag. Experts use these tools in computer forensic investigations to catch bad guys doing bad things. For example, TrueActive is a security company that markets keyboard loggers to law enforcement agencies to monitor online crime. Of course, police officers aren't the only ones using it. According to the TrueActive website, "Thousands of business, government, and individual customers have selected TrueActive as the Best and Safest Choice." One has to wonder why an "individual customer" would need a keyboard logger.

As an interesting side note, some of these keyboard loggers are marketed to parents to monitor teen activity online![1] Of course, sometimes it's the teens doing the monitoring. In 2005, a 16-year-old was arrested in Fort Bend, Texas after stealing (and then selling) exams by adding a keyboard logger to his teacher's computer!

3.4 Eliminating Data Grabbers

As with most forms of unwanted software, the best way to eliminate data grabbers is to avoid them in the first place. For defense, you also want to do the following:

- As always, install a top-rated antivirus package and make sure that you keep it up to date.

- Verify that your antivirus software also checks for spyware and adware. If it doesn't, upgrade to the version that does.

- Download safely! Use common sense, and the questions provided in the next section, to keep your downloads as safe and hassle free as possible.

- Check your machine for preexisting adware and spyware. Remove it promptly.

- Use a commercial (adware-free) download program.

3.4.1 Downloading Safely

Before you decide to install anything on your computer, take into consideration what that means to the big picture. If you are going to be out there downloading, you will eventually get dumped on. Understand what you are agreeing to. Don't close your eyes and agree to something because it will get you somewhere fast. Here are the top five questions to ask:

- Will adware get dumped on my computer? (Not sure? Carefully READ the End User License Agreement!)

- Will this application slow down my computer and steal bandwidth?

---

1. A 2005 study by Pew Internet & American Life Project found that 54% of parents with home Internet access use monitoring software, and 66% of them actually check what theirs kids have been up to online. (Interestingly, only 33% of those teens thought their parents were really monitoring them.)

- Can the site be trusted?

- Can I trust the software I'm downloading?

- It this software really free? Or, am I paying for it by selling my time to watch ads?

3.4.2 Removing Programs

If you find that your machine has already fallen victim to adware or spyware, your first line of defense is to use the Remove Programs feature of your operating system. This function lists most programs that have been installed on your PC and gives you the option to remove them. In most versions of Windows, simply do the following:

1. Click the **Start** button.

2. Select **Control Panel**.

3. Select **Add or Remove Programs**.

If the adware or spyware program you are looking for is not listed, this is a good indication that a high-risk program was dumped and installed without your knowledge. Sometimes, the program will be listed but removing it still won't help. This happens because some adware and spyware companies place two copies of their software on your machine. This means that you can actually delete the software and find that it's still running because you removed only the obvious copy.

3.4.3 Don't Mess with the Registry!

One of the reasons that adware and spyware can be so difficult to remove is that those programs often make numerous changes to the **Windows registry**.

The registry is a database on your computer that controls many aspects of your system, such as user profiles, configuration settings, and application settings. These are incredibly important settings. Make mistakes by changing the wrong things in your registry and you can destroy your system. Your data files will still be there, but your system won't boot. You may need to reinstall the entire system.

Windows Registry A database that defines the settings for Windows itself and many of the application programs installed on your computer.

Modifying or editing the registry is risky business, and rarely worth the risk unless you really know what you are doing! Most antivirus companies provide removal tools within hours after serious outbreaks, so it's far better to wait a bit and get the tools from the experts.

View of Part of the Windows Registry for Windows XP

If you are becoming a serious coder and want to read more about the registry, many books on the market can teach you how to get into the registry and make changes without destroying your system. Still, tread *very* carefully. You're better off purchasing a product that will remove these high-risk unwanted programs.

Chapter 4

Spy vs. Spy

The Helpful Hacker

Like many hackers, Adrian Lamo started early. He actually dates his first "hack" to grade school—a tricky technique to double-write an old disk on the computer he had when he was 8. Double-writing was a neat trick that allowed users to store twice as much information on a diskette. By 18, Adrian was on his own and making quite a name in the hacker community.

Adrian's specialty was breaking into the computer networks of top American companies—America Online, Microsoft, Excite@Home, Yahoo!, World-Com, etc. Dubbed the "helpful hacker" by the media, Adrian didn't take advantage of these break-ins. Instead, he reported his exploits to the network administrators of his victims (and sometimes, also to the press).

By 2001, when he was still only 20, Adrian told a SecurityFocus reporter that his major problem was, "I'm running out of major U.S. corporations." Sadly, that really wasn't his only problem.

When the *New York Times* fell victim to Adrian's skill in 2002, they didn't say, "Thanks!" They pressed charges. Eventually, Adrian was sentenced to 2 years' probation and ordered to pay restitution of over $64,000. Having faced up to 5 years behind bars, he got off easy.

Like Adrian, many hackers don't really expect to be prosecuted. Others just don't expect to be caught. The types and intentions of hackers have been changing. In the past, hackers defaced websites simply because they thought it was fun and because they could get away with it. Today, hackers are financially and even politically motivated. In this chapter, you'll learn about the types of hackers and the tools that hackers use. I'll also discuss how you can learn more about security issues and careers in computer security.

4.1 Hackers

Many teens put their computer skills to use in hacking games—prowling the Internet for shortcuts and ways to "cheat" their favorite computer games.

> *Lawmakers have tightened up statutes to include computer crimes.*

While people use the same term, *hacking* computers is MUCH different than *hacking* games. Hacking a game by using a cheat is something most teens do to figure out the game. It's not a crime to use cheats to beat a game. Hacking a computer without authorization of the owner *is* a crime. Don't think it's cool simply because Hollywood puts a glamorous spin on it, like in the movie *The NET*. Consider Juju Jiang, an 18-year-old from Queens, New York. In February 2005, Juju Jiang was sentenced to 27 months for installing keyboard loggers at a Kinko's copy center and using the passwords logged to access victims' bank accounts. The convictions continue, and the sentences are becoming more serious. In late 2004, Brian Salcedo got 9 years for breaking into Lowe's national computer system and installing software to steal customer's credit card numbers.

While early hackers (particularly teens) got off relatively easy, that trend is turning as the public becomes more aware of the actual costs of computer crime. Lawmakers have also tightened up statutes to include computer crimes. As one prosecutor, U.S. Attorney John McKay, said, "Let there be no mistake about it, cyber-hacking is a crime."

4.1.1 What Is A Hacker?
In general usage, a **hacker** is someone who breaks into someone else's computer system without permission.

Hacker   A programmer who breaks into someone else's computer system without permission.

Some experts like to use the term **cracker** instead, like a safe cracker, because *hacker* can also have other meanings. For example, some programmers like to call themselves hackers and claim that hacking is just coming up with especially clever programming techniques. There's some truth to this, but once Hollywood got hold of the term *hacker*, the media didn't let go.

So long as the general public thinks of hackers as computer criminals, there's not much use trying to redefine the word. For this reason, when I talk about people who break into computer systems in this book, I refer to them as *hackers*.

In the early years, most hackers were computer geeks—usually computer science students—and often fit the profile of brilliant loners seeking to make a name for themselves. We talked about script kiddies in Chapter 2, "Drive-By Malicious Code." Don't forget that not all hackers have talent. Script kiddies are low-talent hackers who use easy, well-known techniques to exploit Internet security vulnerabilities. In the hacker community, being called a script kiddie is a serious insult. Hackers come from all walks of life—from teens who don't realize they are breaking the law, to teens who are trying to show off their stuff. Others are former employees trying to get even with a company they feel wronged them. Still others are part of organized crime rings.

A current fear among law enforcement agencies is the emergence of **cyber-terrorists**. In our post-9/11 world, governments are beginning to realize just how much damage could be done to world economies if one or more outlaw groups were to fly the technological equivalent of a jet plane into the information highway. In theory, a cyber-terrorist could cause substantial damage by shutting down the world economy (literally crashing the computers that run the world's financial markets) or, more likely, by attacking infrastructure through computers that run our heating systems, power plants, hospitals, water purification systems, financial systems, etc. When you consider just how technologically dependent most first-world nations are, the possibilities for disaster become nearly endless.

Cyber-terrorist A hacker or virus writer who uses virus, worm, or coordinated computer attacks to commit an act of terrorism against a political adversary.

While the Internet has yet to fend off a major terrorist attack, the potential for damage is staggering. Governments are taking notice. In 2002, the U.S. House of Representatives overwhelmingly approved the Cyber Security Enhancement Act, a bill that (among many other things) provided for life sentences for hackers convicted of cyber-terrorist activities. While that particular bill died in the U.S. Senate, portions survived and were included in a later Homeland Security bill. While the fate of any piece of legislation is uncertain, it is certain that cyber-terrorism will remain a serious threat for the foreseeable future.

4.1.2 White Hats, Black Hats, and Gray Hats

When it comes to security, there are good guys, bad guys, and another set of guys who live in the middle—called white hats, black hats, and gray hats, respectively. Since there are an awful lot of shades of gray, it's not always as easy as you would think to tell the difference.

White Hats

"White hats" is the name used for security experts. While they often use the same tools and techniques as the black hats, they do so in order to foil the bad guys. That is, they use those tools for ethical hacking and computer forensics. **Ethical hacking** is the process of using security tools to test and improve security (rather than to break it!). **Computer forensics** is the process of collecting evidence needed to identify and convict computer criminals.

Black Hats

Black hats are the bad guys. These are the people who break into computer systems, steal data, shut down networks, and basically commit electronic crimes. We talk about black hats at several points in this book. Black hats and virus writers are not considered the same thing in the security community—even thought they both are breaking the law.

Ethical Hacking Using security tools to find security holes to test and improve security.

Some white hats work for computer security firms. This includes firms that defend companies from computer attacks as well as companies such as Camelot Computer Forensics that help victims of computer crime to successfully prosecute the perpetrators. Camelot, like American Data Recovery (ADR) and Computer Evidence, Ltd., even provides an Expert Witness Program. Given the rise in computer crimes, computer forensics has become a quickly growing career option. Other white hats are specialty programmers employed by major companies and organizations. The job of those white hats is to deploy security solutions and to close up security holes to protect their employers from the black hats, competitors, known threats, and threats on the horizon.

Computer Forensics The process of collecting digital evidence needed to identify and convict computer criminals.

A surprising number of white hats also work for law enforcement agencies. In 2000, Montana joined the ranks of states aggressively pursuing computer criminals when its Justice Department opened a Computer Crime Unit in its Division of Criminal Investigation. On a national level, computer crime falls under the Computer Crime and Intellectual Property Section (CCIPS) of the U.S. Department of Justice. All of these agencies use white hats in one capacity or another.

Gray Hats

Gray hats sit in the middle of the fence because sometimes they cross that ethical line (or more often, define it differently). For example, gray hats may be used to break into a company, wander around their network, leave, go to another company, and wander around their network to see what they can find. They think that simply because they were wandering without doing any damage that they did not break the law. Then they go and get a job as a security consultant for a large corporation. They justify that breaking in and wandering around someone's network was simply done for fun. How would you feel if a stranger came into your house and looked in your closet and all of your dresser drawers. Although the invader never took anything, he looked at everything. It's still an invasion of privacy, and it's still breaking and entering. Right? Well, can you trust gray hats enough to hire them?

> **Hats for All!**
>
> Want a view of all the hats in one room? Try DEFCON. Each July, hackers of all stripes and sizes make their way to Las Vegas for the meeting that bills itself as "the largest underground hacking event open to teens in the world."
>
> Teens who can pony up the $80 registration fee are welcome to the event. *PC World* dubbed DEFCON as "School for Hackers"—an extravaganza of hacking tips, hacker news, and more.
>
> In 2004, nearly 1,800 "hackers" showed up for the event. Of course, so did the good guys. In fact, "Spot the Fed" has become a rather popular conference game, where the hackers point out the FBI agents sitting in the audience.

4.2 Hackers Want Your PC

You might be thinking that hackers don't care about your computer, but they do. Hackers want access to your system for many different reasons. For example, we talked about "bot" networks and armies of "bot" networks in Chapter 2. The more systems that hackers have under their control, the better off they are. Once your system is compromised and connected into one of these armies, some hackers sell your system's name on a list of compromised PCs. Remember, once a hacker breaks in and plants a Trojan, the door is open for *anyone* to return. The hackers know this and are making money off of it. They know it's easy to hide and very difficult to track back to the hackers once they own your PC.

The Internet is an easy place to hide. Compromised computers around the world have helped to make hiding simple. It is easy to find the last **IP address** from where an attack was launched, but hackers hop from many unsecured systems to hide their location before they launch attacks.

IP Address   A unique address that identifies where a computer is connected to the Internet.

Over the past three years, most cyber-attacks have been launched from computers within the United States. However, this doesn't mean that systems in the United States are the original source of these attacks. A hacker in Russia could actually use your computer to launch a denial-of-service (DoS) attack. To the world, it might even look as if you started the attack because the hacker has hidden his tracks so that only the last "hop" can be traced.

A determined hacker can use any one of those PCs to launch an attack.

4.3 Hacker Tools

In the old days, hackers would pass around tools in the underground. Today, hackers offer free tools all over the Internet. For an eyeful, try asking Google to search for free hacker tools (see **Figure 4.1**).

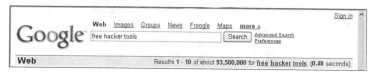

Figure 4.1
Searching for hacker tools

Granted, all 20-million-plus hits aren't necessarily to the actual tools, but more than enough of them can spread some serious mischief.

Learning about these tools is important, but so is the way that you learn. Trying them out in a supervised lab or computer class is fine, but don't be tempted to test them out on the Internet on your own. Unless, of course, you don't mind being arrested, getting your parents into a lawsuit, or going to jail.

Remember, hacking into a computer is against the law. Before taking a hacker tool from the Internet, ask yourself, "Can I trust hacker tools?" Some hacker tools open up backdoors so that the hackers can get into *your* system.

4.3.1 Scanning Tools

Scanning tools are used by white hats to test security over the network. A good scanning tool will scan an Internet-connected computer for a wide range of security vulnerabilities. It might use "port scanning" to see whether or not your computer's

Internet connection is well guarded. It will also check which operating system you're running and look to see whether you've applied patches to the known security holes in that system. And, of course, it will give your firewall a workout, testing that your machine is protected from a wide variety of outside attacks.

Of course, white hats aren't the only people who can make use of scanning tools. To scan your own system, try Shields Up, a free scanning tool available from Gibson Research Company at http://www.grc.com (see **Figure 4.2**). Other companies offer free scans, including Symantec.com and McAfee.com. I like GRC.com the most because it provides good information on how to fix your security problems. You don't need to download a thing; simply click on Shields Up to get a quick look at how your security stacks up.

Figure 4.2

Free security testing

4.3.2 Password Cracking

Password crackers are among the most common and elementary tools in the hacker toolkit. These have been around for some time and are fairly effective at "guessing" most users' passwords, at least in part because most users do a very poor job of selecting secure passwords.

The first step to password cracking is often simple guesswork. This is made easy by social engineering. Hackers are just as aware as system administrators that users prefer to select simple passwords that are easy to remember. The top choices are nearly always names that are personally meaningful to the user—first names of immediate family members lead the list, followed by pet's names and favorite sporting teams. Password crackers may end up loading full English (and often Spanish) dictionaries, but they can hit a fair number of passwords with the contents of any popular baby name book. Other poor password selections include common numbers and numbers that follow a common format, such as phone numbers and social security numbers.

> **Forgot Your Password?**
>
> Join the club. So have 8 out of 10 computer users!

The key to creating a **good password** is to create something that someone cannot guess or easily crack. Using your pet's name, therefore, is *not* a good technique. Putting your password on a sticky note and pasting it to your computer is a bad idea, too. Also, using your login name is a bad technique because someone who knows your login may just try it for your password and thus get into your system.

Automated password-cracking tools have been around for a decade. These tools look for common names, words, and combined words. Therefore, one of the best methods is to use non-words with special characters to create a password. Many applications require seven or eight characters. To create an ideal password, make sure it contains at least seven characters, use both numbers and letters, throw in at least one capital letter (since most passwords are case-sensitive), and include a special symbol such as *, $, or #. For the letter portion, you can combine words that mean something to you but would be difficult to crack. For example, my house is number 18, my pet's name is Vegas, and I love to look at the stars at night. So a good password for me to remember (but a hard one for hackers to crack) would be Vegas18*. Don't be lazy and get stuck in the habit of using weak passwords.

Good Passwords   These are non-words created by combining things you can remember, such as combining your pet's name, your street address, and a symbol.

Another important rule is NOT to use the same password for multiple accounts. For heavy computer users, this is an awfully hard rule to follow. Users who don't rely on multiuse passwords often rely on other equally unsecure methods to remember all of them. They write them down on sticky notes (a major security risk in a public access environment). They choose simple passwords that are easy to remember (and easy to crack). Or, they simply forget their passwords.

Since the major problem with setting passwords is users' inability to remember secure passwords, it is unlikely that this problem will abate until passwords are replaced with easier forms of technology, such as **biometrics**. Biometrics is the use of secure biological data for identification. Common biometric systems use fingerprints, voice recognition, and retinal (eye) scans. The great advantage to these systems is that users can't forget them, it's nearly impossible to accidentally (or deliberately) pass them on to another person, and they're incredibly difficult to fake. For now, however, biometric systems are too expensive to be used widely.

Biometrics   The use of biological data, such as fingerprints or retinal scans, for identification.

Eventually, those prices will drop. Sony currently markets a Windows-compatible fingerprint reader called Puppy for under $100. That's still too high to entice most users to switch from free keyboard entry of passwords, but it is a sign that prices are moving in the right direction. In the meantime, you'll need to be smart about creating passwords. You might also want to educate your parents on how to create a safe and easy-to-remember password since they might have financial and personal information at risk.

4.3.3 Rootkit

The ultimate goal for a hacker is to own total control of your system without your knowledge. A **rootkit** is a type of malicious code that can make that happen. Specifically, a rootkit is a collection of tools that a hacker uses to do two things:

- Gain full access to a compromised computer or computer network

- Hide the fact that the machine or network has been compromised

The first rootkits were created in the early 1990s. Since then, they've become very sophisticated. Today's rootkits open new backdoors for further access, collect user names and passwords, install and monitor keyboard loggers, and even attack other machines or networks. Rootkits even alter log files to hide the fact that the files were compromised and disable security software. Using these tools, rootkits can run in a way that they are fully trusted. They can hide from other software running on the system, and they can escape detection by the programs used to monitor the system behavior.

Rootkit   A collection of tools that allows a hacker to gain full access of a vulnerable computer and hide his tracks.

So how does a rootkit arrive? Usually in one of two ways. The most common route is through an open security hole (such as an unpatched operating system vulnerability) that allows the hacker to break into the target machine in the first place. Rootkits can also arrive via worms.

Some pretty serious computer attacks have been accomplished using rootkits. Just take a look at the University of Connecticut. In June 2005, university officials admitted that they'd discovered a rootkit that had been installed—and run undetected—on one of their **servers** since 2003. The "rooted" server had contained personal information on a large number of students, staff, and faculty. While there was no evidence that the intrusion had resulted in specific thefts of identity, this left the university in the position of notifying 72,000 people that their names, social security numbers, birth dates, and telephone numbers might have been stolen.

Server A computer that "serves" a larger system (like a mainframe computer) by providing high-speed access to specific types of data, such as personal files or email accounts.

No doubt other servers have been hit just as hard. As Mark Russinovich, co-founder of the Sysinternals.com site, told *eWeek*, "My guess is that there have been other discoveries in other places but we just haven't heard about this." Russinovich, who offers a free utility called Rootkit Revealer, expects to see the use of rootkits explode.

4.4 Calling White Hats!

With recent increases in computer crimes, and the decisions by law enforcement to treat computer crimes more seriously, there has come a growing shortage of white hats. Since supply and demand determine price, salaries are on the rise as well. Aiming high on the food chain? In 2004, *ComputerWorld* put the price of Chief Security Officers at over $100,000 per year. Even better is the outlook for employment. While hiring in the tech world has remained flat for several years now, security jobs often go begging.

There's a lot to say for being a white hat. In addition to great employment options and salaries, there's the bonus of knowing that you're helping to make the Internet a better and safer place.

If you're considering a career in computer security, look for colleges and universities that offer computer security as part of the computer-science curriculum. Purdue University in Indiana, in particular, has had some famous white hats graduate from its program. But it's hardly the only option. Since 2000, the number of colleges, universities, and trade schools offering computer security programs has tripled.

To learn more about careers in computer security, ethical hacking, and security tools, have a look at some of these security sites:

- **SecurityFocus** (http://securityfocus.com/) is an independent site, not affiliated with any specific security product. SecurityFocus provides extensive up-to-date information about computer security to meet the needs of computer users and information technology professionals.

- **SearchSecurity.com** (http://searchsecurity.techtarget.com/) is a full-service site aimed at computer security professionals. This site provides a security-specific search engine, daily security news, sign-up options for security-related email newsletters, and over a thousand links to other security sites.

- **SANS.org** (http://www.sans.org/) is the official site of the SANS (SysAdmin, Audit, Network, Security) Institute, a world leader in computer security training. SANS provides many free resources, including weekly digests of security risks (@RISK) and general security news (NewsBites), as well over 1,000 technical papers on computer security.

- **CERIAS** (http://www.cerias.purdue.edu/) is the Center for Education and Research in Information Assurance and Security. Run through Purdue University, the CERIAS website provides a wide range of information related to computer security issues.

4.5 Finding and Reporting the Holes

Reporting security problems to the public has several serious implications. First, it really does spur companies with security problems in their products to pony up the fixes fast. But, it does so at a price. When the general public is informed about a major security risk, so are the legions of black hats. While the software manufacturer is in overdrive trying to fix the problem, hackers are in overdrive trying to exploit the vulnerability before the fixes hit the Net.

When the general public is informed about a major security risk, so are the legions of black hats.

Imagine for a moment that your brother left your parents' house unlocked before you left for your family vacation last summer. Without thinking, you mentioned this to a stranger, who then drove back to your hometown and robbed the house. Was the cause of that robbery the unlocked door or the unthinking comment? That's hard to say. Now let's assume that you mentioned this problem deliberately and you did so at a club known to be frequented by thieves. Is the robbery still your brother's fault? Yes, but it is certainly your fault as well.

The same logic applies to the tactics. Some security researchers claim to publicize faults to prevent future crime. Still, they're well aware that the black hats will do everything in their power to take advantage of that information before a fix is available. The end result? Important information is at risk, maybe even your parent's medical records or financial information.

Chapter 5

Giving Spam the Curb

The Great Spam Monster

Tessa was thrilled during the Easter holidays when her dad finally let her open her own email account. She checked it four to five times a day—eager to have mail of her own. Every day it seemed she was giving her new address to someone else—friends at school, kids from her church youth group, even new friends she'd met in online chat rooms. To make sure that everyone could find her, she added her name to online directories and even posted her new address on her family's web page.

The first month or so, everything was wonderful. Tessa felt connected to the world. Then she started to hear from some of its darker inhabitants.

First, Tessa began getting boring stupid emails intended for grownups. Silly people trying to sell her stuff no real 13-year-old could possibly want. Some of them even tried to get her to sign up for credit cards. Tessa tried to get rid of the emails, sending replies to links that were supposed to remove her from the mailing lists. The number of emails just kept on increasing.

After a while, the mail Tessa was getting got creepy. And again, the number of emails kept rising. By the last week of school, Tessa was getting so much junk email or spam, that she couldn't find the messages from her friends in the pile. She gave up and quit using her email.

As summer started, Tessa's dad signed her up for a new email account. This time, he defined filters to automatically throw away the messages she wouldn't want. Now, Tessa's being very careful who she gives her new email address to.

Like Tessa, most teens are overwhelmed by email they don't want and really shouldn't have to see.[1] Teens aren't the only ones uncomfortable either. The sheer number of unsolicited email messages wastes incredible amounts of computer resources. Most Internet users receive more spam messages than messages from friends, employers, and family put together.

5.1 Email and Spam

Spam is the electronic equivalent of junk mail. That's email you didn't ask for (or you agreed to accept without realizing) and almost always don't want. Some spam is junk email from legitimate companies trying to sell you their products. Others are junk email from less-than-respectable companies trying to do the same. Taken together, all those spammers eat up a ton of bandwidth.[2]

5.1.1 What Is Spam?

If you're curious, SPAM is actually a canned meat product. If you haven't had it, the taste is somewhere in between ham and corned beef. However, in computer usage the term spam comes from an early 1970s comedy skit by a British comedy troupe called Monty Python. In the skit, a couple is trying to order breakfast without SPAM in a restaurant where every meal comes with SPAM in some form. The overall feeling is that SPAM is everywhere, in everything, and you just can't escape it. Junk email definitely generates the same feelings.

---

1. According to a 2003 study by Applied Research, 80% of computer users 18 and under were receiving inappropriate spam. Over a third had received email messages that made them feel uncomfortable.
2. A 2005 study by MX Logic Inc., a company that makes email protection software, found that 67% of the email its products processed was spam.

Spam   Unsolicited email messages, also called electronic junk mail.

Most Internet users receive more spam messages than messages from friends, employers, and family put together.

A surprising amount of spam is for products that are either clearly illegal or on pretty shaky ground. At the risk of being obvious, any college degree that you can get over the Internet while attending no classes and taking no tests of any kind is clearly not cool. This type of company is called a diploma mill. A diploma issued by such a school is not a real college degree. More important, using such a fake diploma to get a job or obtain a promotion is illegal. Whether this particular ad is illegal or not is questionable because they include the term *non-accredited*. In academic circles, "accredited" means a real, accepted university. There are several accrediting groups that go around and make sure that colleges and universities meet certain requirements in order to issue valid college degrees. If an institution doesn't meet those requirements, it becomes a "non-accredited" school. Such a school can continue to print diplomas, but they don't actually mean anything.

Another common source of spam is ads for online degree programs. In fairness, there are a number of excellent, highly respected online degree programs— particularly for master's degrees. However, most of these schools don't flood the Net with spam advertising their programs. The schools that do tend to be—you guessed it—"non-accredited" universities. In evaluating any item or service you find advertised in unsolicited email, remember "Caveat Emptor." That's Latin for "Let the buyer beware!"

5.1.2 Isn't Spam Illegal?
That's a good question without an easy answer. Truthfully, some spam is illegal. Some isn't. It's also very difficult to tell the difference. Because spam is so disruptive, the U.S. Congress addressed it specifically in the CAN-SPAM Act of 2003. Like most government initiatives, this name is an acronym—CAN-SPAM actually stands for Controlling the Assault of Non-Solicited Pornography and Marketing.

Giving Spam the Curb

Have lawmakers been effective in giving spam the curb? Hardly. Giving spam the curb takes more than laws. Spammers don't play by the rules. They use spoofed email addresses, web bugs, email scavengers, and do just about anything to get valid email addresses.

While its goal was to reduce the amount of spam by making senders legally liable, the bill wasn't terribly effective. In fact, its definitions actually legalized a good bit of spam, leading opponents to begin calling it the "I Can Spam" Act. What the bill did define as illegal was any unsolicited electronic messages that didn't include a valid subject line and header, the real postal address of the mailer, a clear label marking the content as adult-only if it was, and an opt-out mechanism.

The big problem with CAN-SPAM was the opt-out mechanism. An opt-out mechanism is a way for the recipient to get off the mailing list. You've no doubt seen these in junk email that you've received. The general format is:

```
If you would prefer not to receive further information from Spammer-of-Your-Choice,
please reply back to this message with "Remove" in the subject line.
```

You may also have seen this format:

```
If you would like to stop receiving our advertisements or believe this message was sent
in error, you can visit our subscription management page.
```

To add more substance to their claims of legitimacy, spammers often actually cite the CAN-SPAM act in their opt-out clauses:

```
This email is a commercial advertisement sent in compliance with the CANSPAM Act of
2003. We have no desire to send you information that is not wanted, therefore, if you
wish to be excluded from future mailings, please use the link at the bottom of the page.
```

The general idea is always the same. To get off the mailing list, you need to visit the spammer's website or send them an email. The problem is that as soon as you do so, you have verified that they have a real, valid email address and that their messages are getting through. If the spammer plays by the rules, this works well. If they don't, you have just told them that your email address is worth selling. Because many spammers don't play by the rules, experts strongly recommend that you NEVER reply to unsolicited email or visit links included in spam. Doing so can greatly increase, rather than decrease, the amount of spam you receive in the future.

5.2 Spoofing

A spoof is a parody of something familiar. In its pure form, a spoof is usually a pretty good joke. Weird Al Yankovic has made a career out of writing musical spoofs of popular songs. One of his best was a 1983 parody of Michael Jackson's hit "Beat It" called "Eat It." The music video for this one was especially funny.

Spoofing addresses are not so funny. **Spoofing** happens when the person who sends you an email pretends to be someone else. Spammers are able to "spoof" messages by defining fake headers that include phony routing information. Real routing information is the part of your email that defines your email accounts' Internet address. These are the numbers that allow email servers to deliver your mail. You can think of the routine definition as very much like a postal address. If the address isn't valid, the email doesn't get through. Phony routing information hides the real address of the person sending an email message.

5.2.1 Spoofed Addresses

When you send an email message to someone else, the message sent always begins with a header that includes your name and email address. Those items are defined in your email software as the "Display name" and "Display email address." By changing those settings, you can actually display anything you want. Spammers also insert fake routing information; this makes it appear that the email was sent through one or more systems that most likely never touched it. Tracing messages spoofed with fake routing information is MUCH more difficult and sometimes impossible.

Spoofed Email An email message containing a fake or forged "From:" address, making it difficult and sometimes impossible to tell where it was actually sent from.

One of the reasons that spoofing email is fairly easy is because email headers are created using SMTP (Simple Mail Transfer Protocol), and SMTP lacks authentication. One way to limit spoofing is to use digital signatures with your email. We'll talk about that in Chapter 14, "Tweaks."

SMTP (Simple Mail Transfer Protocol)   The Internet rules used to send and create email messages.

In some cases, spoofed emails are simply amusing. A few years ago, I received a very funny election parody that appeared to have come from the Democratic National Headquarters. It was clearly a joke and the spoofing (while inappropriate) wasn't done in malice. That's not the case for many spoofed emails.

Phishing   A con artist scam using spoofed email messages to trick people into giving out personal and financial information.

Spoofed addresses are a common theme in phishing attempts. **Phishing** (pronounced "fishing") is a con-artist trick to fish for information. Phishers send email that appears to come from a company you know and trust, and they ask for information that you would probably want that company to have. At the moment, users of online services such as eBay, Amazon, and PayPal are often the targets of phishers. For example, if you or your parents enjoy buying items on auction at eBay, you probably have a PayPal account. PayPal allows you to create an online bank account and use that account to buy items on eBay without giving your credit card number to the eBay sellers. If you have a PayPal account, you've probably already received an email similar to the one shown in **Figure 5.1**.

Figure 5.1
Spoofed email

The problem? This particular email message was *not* sent by PayPal. If you click the included links and enter the information they request, you will be literally giving your parent's credit card information to thieves.

We'll talk more about phishing in Chapter 7, "Phishing for Dollars." For now, just be aware that when it comes to email headers, don't think just because it looks like it came from a real company that it actually did.

5.2.2 SPAM Proxies and Relays

As you now know, much of the spam that is circulating didn't really come from the addresses contained in those emails. What you don't know is that some of it may even have come from your machine.

How can that happen? In Chapter 2, "Drive-By Malicious Code," we talked about bot armies and how malicious code writers can infect your PC with a Trojan program that turns it into a bot (also called a **zombie**). A lot of those zombies are used to send spam. One virus that does this is SoBig.F. Like many email worms, SoBig also spoofs the addresses in the emails it sends so that they appear to come from someone else whose address appears in your email address book.

When a zombie PC is hijacked and used to send spam, it's called a **spam relay**. That PC is simply "relaying" (passing on) spam messages that originated somewhere else. This happens a lot. A 2005 study by MX Logic found that 40% of the spam it identified was being sent by hijacked machines infected with Trojans that turned them into spam relays.[3]

Spam Relay   A PC that has been hijacked into a bot network and is being used to send spam without the PC owner's knowledge.

While home PCs are definitely a problem, sometimes so are the mail servers used by Internet Service Providers (ISPs). While fewer servers than individual PCs are hijacked, their extensive databases of email addresses still make them a large problem. When a mail server is hijacked to send spam, it's called a **spam proxy**.

---

3. Other examiners put that figure much higher. In 2004, network equipment manufacturer Sandvine claimed that 80% of spam was being routed through compromised home computers. While some experts thought that number too high, all agreed that unprotected home computers are a major stumbling block in the fight against spam.

SPAM Proxy An email server that has been hijacked to deliver spam.

Today, ISPs are taking great care to prevent their mail servers from being hijacked. Tragically, most home PC users are not. Luckily, the steps needed to protect your machine from being turned into a spam relay are the same as the steps required to protect yourself from computer viruses, worms, and Trojans.

5.3 Knock, Knock— How Spammers Know You're Home

Assuming that you haven't been posting your email address all over the Internet, you may be wondering how the spammers find you and why they send you so MANY email messages. That's a good question with a couple of good answers.

5.3.1 Hidden Tracking

Popular belief has it that in the event of a nuclear meltdown, the two groups virtually guaranteed to survive are rats and cockroaches. This probably applies to the Internet as well. In the event of a total system shutdown, the first groups to resurface are likely to be spammers (rats) and web bugs (cockroaches).

If you haven't seen a **web bug**, or even heard of one, you're in the majority. A web bug (sometimes called a **web beacon**) is a hidden image that spammers use to track email messages. In technical terms, most web bugs are defined as a transparent GIF (a picture file) having a size of only 1×1 pixel, making them much too small to actually see in an email.

Web Bug A hidden image that spammers use to verify that you're actually reading the spam they sent you. (Also called a **web beacon** or **transparent GIF**.)

When you read an email message, graphics or picture elements in the email are displayed by being downloaded from a separate website. In the past, most email programs were set to automatically download graphics so readers had no idea they were downloading information from another site. Today, that default has been reset so that you'll often see broken images, as shown in **Figure 5.2**. You need to right-click to download the images, thus alerting the spammer that the email has been read.

Right-click here to download pictures. To help protect your privacy, Outlook prevented automatic download of this picture fro

Right-click here to download pictures. To help protect your privacy, Outlook prevented automatic download of this picture from the Internet.

Figure 5.2
Preventing automatic downloads

5.3.2 Scavengers and Crawlers

I said that you might be surprised by the amount of spam you get, assuming that you hadn't posted your email address all over the Internet. Amazingly, many people do just that! They use their email addresses as user names for online communities, include their email addresses on their websites, and even use their actual addresses when posting messages to online user groups. All of these steps are good ways to get spam.

Email Scavenger   A type of web crawler program that searches the Internet and collects (harvests) all the email addresses it finds posted on web pages.

One by One...

When you look at a picture on your computer screen, you see a solid graphic image—much like a photograph or drawing. In reality, each computer image is composed of thousands of tiny little dots, called pixels.

The term *pixel*, in fact, is an abbreviation for "picture element." How many pixels a graphic has determines its resolution—how "solid" or crisp the picture looks.

If you use a digital camera, you already understand this term. A high-quality photograph takes an awful lot of pixels. For example, the Kodak EasyShare P880 provides an 8 megapixel sensor. That's eight times roughly 1 million pixels for a single photograph.

Backing up, try to imagine a picture that's only 1 pixel by 1 pixel. You can't see it, which is of course, the idea of web bug graphics.

Posting your email address online can cause problems because some spammers use programs to crawl web pages (i.e., search them) on the Internet looking for the famous @ sign, which appears in nearly every email address. Some companies earn fairly decent profits by doing just this. Ada Email Address Search XP Pro claims to search and harvest email addresses from over 3 billion web pages. At $79.95 a pop for licensing fees, this is a nice moneymaker for them. Other companies sell the service of sending unsolicited email on your behalf to their own extensive lists. How extensive? Email Marketing Center claims to maintain lists of 50-million-plus addresses with new additions daily. Their best deal at the moment is 15 million emails for only $12.95. No wonder spam is filling up so many Inboxes!

5.3.3 Is Your Email Address for Sale?

Probably. If your email address has been posted on the Internet, chances are that someone is selling it right now. Because the Net is a public place, harvesting addresses for sale (although annoying) is a perfectly legal endeavor. Of course, not all sales of email addresses are legal.

Why bother? There's quite a bit of money involved. Consider the stolen AOL customer list. In June 2004, a now former software engineer at AOL, Jason Smathers, was arrested for selling a list containing 92 million AOL screen names to spammer Sean Dunaway. Smathers got $28,000 (and subsequently 15 months in prison) for the initial list. Dunaway, in turn, not only used the list to send spam for his Internet gambling firm, he sold it to other spammers for $52,000.

5.4 Social Engineering

We've talked about why people get spammed; the next question is why those same people open the messages. This brings us back to a concept we discussed earlier, social engineering.

> **Most messages rely on social engineering to trick recipients into reading their email.**

Most messages rely on social engineering to trick recipients into reading their email. These are some of the same tricks that virus writers use to get you to open email attachments when you know you really shouldn't.

For social engineering purposes, spammers rely heavily on the displayed From: and Subject: fields in the email messages. Often, From: fields are spoofed to appear to come from companies or organizations you know and trust. The Subject: lines are written to catch you off-guard or play on curiosity or greed.

Here are some of the more common subject lines that spammers use:

```
Subject:  RE: About your email
```

This approach tries to catch you off-guard and trick you into thinking that this message is a response to an email you sent. Don't assume that every email that begins RE: is really a reply. Always look at the Sender: field.

```
Subject:  Free Xbox games for 30 days
Subject:  Sweepstakes PRIZE Notification — You WON!!!!
```

Free stuff is always great, isn't it? Since many teens enter online sweepstakes and contests, this is a very effective approach. When you receive an email like this, ask yourself whether the prize matches up with any sweepstakes you really entered. You also might want to be careful about entering all those sweepstakes. Many exist solely to harvest email addresses.

```
Subject: Lose up to 50 pounds in one month!
```

According to the latest weigh-ins, nearly half of Americans could fall for this one. Unfortunately, most products advertised via spam are more likely to lighten your wallet than anything else. The person to ask for weight-loss help is your doctor, not your neighborhood spammer.

5.5 Keeping Spam Out of Your Inbox

When spammers first started gaining ground, there really weren't enough good tools to keep them out. Fortunately, today there are many sophisticated tools and techniques for blocking spam. The way you use your email address and the actions you take when spam gets in are both important components in keeping spam out.

Even though technology to block spam is getting better, spammers are always trying to work their way around it. No method will protect you from 100% of spam. Still, your first line of defense is to do the following:

- Delete suspicious email without reading it! This is a good way to avoid viruses and worms as well as more spam.

- Don't click on links in your email. Remember the web bugs? Don't let them crawl into your PC!

- Don't reply to spam. While a few opt-out mechanisms are really legitimate, an awful lot more of them aren't. In the long run, you'll get less if you just delete it than if you ask to be removed from the mailing list.

- Watch where you post your email address. To avoid being caught by web crawlers collecting email addresses, don't post your full email address on any publicly accessible web page.

- Use filters if you have them, but don't trust them to do the whole job. Filters can be a useful tool in avoiding some types of spam, but they're very limited. Spammers are constantly rewriting their Subject: lines to avoid having their emails being thrown away by filters. Often, message content is contained in a graphic/picture file. Since filters scan text, they miss any key words or phrases contained in graphics.

As a final note on filters, be very careful what you tell them to look for. The early Internet filters used by schools and public libraries to keep out inappropriate content used very specific phrases and keywords to block messages and websites with sexually explicit content. As a result, students searching on school computers really were unable to access inappropriate web pages. They were also unable to access information about breast cancer or even recipes for fried chicken because the word *breast* was included in the filter block. I've also heard of student sports fans unable to complete research on Super Bowl XXX because the roman numerals mimicked a common marker for adult-only sites. When you or your parents enter words and phrases for your own filters, make sure you're not so specific that you filter out stuff you really want.

5.6 SPIM

SPIM is the instant messenger version of spam. Like spam, it proliferates wildly and greatly annoys its recipients. The distribution of SPIM has grown with the use of instant messaging.

SPIM   Unsolicited instant messages. SPIM is the IM version of spam.

Teens use instant messaging even more heavily than adults. As a result, they are even more likely to receive SPIM. Sometimes, that SPIM is even intentionally targeted at teens. In February of 2005, an 18-year-old New Yorker, Anthony Greco, became the first person arrested for sending SPIM after he flooded MySpace.com with roughly 1.5 million SPIM messages. MySpace is an online community (like Xanga) heavily frequented by teens. Anthony literally overwhelmed those users with SPIM ads for mortgage refinancing and inappropriate adult sites. If you're thinking that he couldn't have expected much click-through on the mortgage ads, you may have missed the point. Anthony's real goal wasn't to sell the services being SPIMmed; it was to extort money from MySpace. He actually contacted them and offered to protect their users against SPIM for a mere $150 a day. That turned out not to have been his brightest move. Greco was actually arrested at the Los Angeles airport where he thought he was flying out to meet Tom Anderson, president of MySpace, to sign a payment agreement for the extorted funds. Some criminals just don't think it through!

Chapter 6

Pretenders and Pirates

Mindy and the Mock Money Orders

A typical teenager from Michigan, Mindy spent a lot of time on the Internet—much of that time in chat rooms with online friends. Over a period of 5 months, she spent a lot of time in particular chatting with "George," an online friend from London.

> "I'M 21, AND HAVE LONG BLOND HAIR..."

As she got to know him (or so she thought), Mindy learned that George was having some problems with money. He had tons of money, of course; he was just having a hard time getting access to it. Mindy could fix this for him. All she needed to do was to cash a few money orders and send the cash back to George. Naturally, she should keep a few hundred dollars for her troubles.

A money order is a like a bank check used by people who don't have a bank checking account. You can buy a money order using cash at any post office. Many people use money orders; some Internet businesses such as eBay sellers actually require money orders for payment because it's safer to accept a money order from a stranger than it is to take a bank check. That's because a money order is paid for in cash. It can't "bounce" like a check can if the person's bank account doesn't contain enough money to cover the check.

Knowing that money orders are safe, and truly wanting to help her friend, Mindy agreed to cash the money orders. Luckily for her, the post office realized right away that the money orders were fake. Even luckier for her, they opted to go after George instead of pressing charges against her.

"George," of course, knew full well that the money orders he tricked Mindy into trying to cash were all counterfeit. Not that it's likely that George was his real name. Or that he actually lived in London. Or that any of the myriad details on his life that he provided to Mindy those 5 months were actually true. In real life, George could very well be a 60-year-old woman running a counterfeiting ring from Southeast Asia. About the only "fact" that Mindy knows for sure at this point is that George was most definitely a pretender.

Unfortunately, the Internet is full of pretenders. Some of those pretenders are scam artists, like George. According-ing to postal inspector Fred Van De Putte, the money order scam is especially common. In March of 2005, he noted, "Since December, we have collected in our office in Detroit over $300,000 worth of counterfeit money orders that have come to people primarily by a contact with somebody over the Internet." Other pretenders are iden-tity thieves. Their goal is to get to know you well enough to take over your identity when you're not looking. Other pretenders are even worse—pedophiles pretending to be teens themselves to locate new victims.

> *The fellow "teen" you can really talk to about your life may not even be a teen.*

To avoid becoming a victim, you need to be more aware of just what you can and can't tell about online acquaintances. And, what you should and shouldn't tell to those same people.

6.1 Meeting People Online

The Internet is a wonderful tool for keeping in touch with friends and meeting new people who share your interests and goals. Where else could you find a ready-made community of people who love the same music, collect similar things, or can team up and compete in games with other teens around the world. And for teens look-

ing for support or help, the Internet provides many opportunities for seemingly anonymous help with serious
problems they're too afraid or embarrassed to discuss
at home.

The problem is that people who want to "help" aren't
always what or who they claim to be. The fellow
"teen" you can really talk to about your life may not
even be a teen. Just ask Amy, a 14-year-old Seattle teen.
Amy was having family problems and was thrilled to find
another teen online who understood exactly what she was go-
ing through. After months of Amy baring her soul online, 14-year-old Carl offered
to help her run away. Throwing caution (and common sense) to the wind, Amy
joined Carl on a bus heading to Missouri. The longer they traveled though, the less
sure Amy was about Carl. During a short stop on their route, Amy had the chance
to rummage through Carl's wallet. What she learned was that 14-year-old Carl was
really 27-year-old Robert. Miraculously, she was able to escape his company and
was returned to her parents. As for "Carl," he's probably still out there and still
pretending. Much to the disgust of Amy and her parents, he was never charged.
According to investigators, "luring laws don't apply because she talked with
him willingly."

Amy learned a very hard lesson in an extremely dangerous way. Today, she still
uses the Internet but only under close supervision by her parents. For those times
they're not in, her father has now installed monitoring software and makes it a
point to know who she's talking to and about what.

F2F A face-to-face meeting (in person) with someone you've met online.

Is Amy's story unusual? Yes and no. Taking the risk of meeting online friends F2F
(face to face) is something that few Internet users attempt. The specter of teens
baring their souls to perfect strangers is unfortunately still far too common. Are
you likely to have Amy's awful experience? Probably not. Truthfully, most of the
people you meet online really are who and what they claim to be. But the reality is
that just as creeps exist in real life, those same creeps exist online. Are they hiding

behind every other screen name? Hardly. But there are enough of them out there that you need to understand just how easy it is for them to lie and hide behind a digital face because you can't see them.

6.1.1 Where Pretenders Hang Online

There's a common fallacy that pretenders spend their time online in racy chat rooms and sleazy online communities. That may be true, but those are certainly not the only places they hang out. Savvy con artists and pedophiles look for easy marks. The more naive their quarry, the better their odds.

Keep this in mind as you chat online, and don't assume that all visitors to "whole-some" forums are themselves wholesome. Fourteen-year-old Amy made exactly that mistake. Explaining why she took Carl at his online face value, she explains, "I assumed because it was a Christian chat room that there would be mostly Christians in there. So, basically it would be like a regular conversation with people." Pretenders generally don't have CREEP figuratively tattooed on their online profiles. They also make it a point to be where they're most likely to find vulnerable teens. So, don't be surprised to find them in church-related chat rooms, online religious communities, scouting-themed groups, and other so called "wholesome" teen forums.

6.1.2 Watch Out for the Fakes

It is easy to meet new people online. Your friends will introduce you to their friends, and their friends, and so on. Before you know it, your digital network is HUGE. It might seem easy to talk to people online because you feel safe. No one is in front of you judging how you look, talk, walk, or part your hair. You can never take meeting someone over the Internet lightly, however. If you don't know that person and were not introduced to that person, you have no idea if this person is who he says he is. You may even feel "connected" to your new friends, but you need to keep in mind that some people lie on the Internet.

An important question to ask is, What kind of lies are being told? Also, how big are those lies? Let's face it, on the Internet people lie about a lot of different things. Age and gender are two big ones. That pretty teenage girl your friend has been hitting on could very well be a 40-year-old man.

Watching out for predators on the Internet comes down to common sense and taking a few precautions:

- **Don't give out personal information.**

  This includes your full name, your home address, and your home phone number. If you're using an online forum or group chat room, you will want to keep your personal email address to yourself as well.

- **Don't participate in conversations that make you uncomfortable.**

  If the discussion turns to topics that make your skin crawl (or even itch), log off and stay off. Remember that the Internet, like the telephone, exists for YOUR convenience. On the phone, if you're being hounded by someone you don't want to talk to, you can use Caller ID to essentially block that person from getting through. You can also do the same thing online.

  Just because someone wants to talk to you doesn't mean that you're obligated to talk to them. Most online communities provide ways to block access to specific members. If you're using Instant Messenger, you can block users you don't want to talk to. Even in email, you can add an address to your spam filters and have your email utility automatically throw away any messages from that address.

- **NEVER tolerate harassment.**

  If those uncomfortable conversations start to feel like harassment, tell your parents and together, report that person to the authorities. Harassing someone online is called *cyberstalking*, and in many states this is actually a crime. It's not something you ever have to put up with.

- **If someone you met online wants to meet you in person, let your parents know.**

  Meeting people in person you met online isn't always dark and evil. As we know from online dating services, some people really do find their soul mates that way. Your parents will have a MUCH better idea than you will whether or not it's safe to meet someone you've met online. If nothing else, they'll be better prepared to verify the person's identity.

If you're serious about meeting someone you "know" from online, be just as serious about verifying that person's identity in advance. If they claim to be active in a nearby town's church group, telephone the rector and ask if that's true. For fellow scouts, check with the leader of their claimed troop. There are lots of ways to verify that someone is really who he says he is. Your parents can be very helpful in this.

- **Absolutely NEVER, EVER meet anyone F2F for the first time by yourself.**

This is pretty self-explanatory but probably the most critical deterrent to online creeps. Don't put yourself in a dangerous situation when you don't need to.

6.2 Digital Neighborhoods

Most of us are taught from a very early age that it is unacceptable to lie. In my house, our teens know that no matter how bad something is that they do, they need to tell their dad and me the truth. Our family is built on truth. That's not always fun, but that's just the way it is in our house. Your house probably runs the same way.

Given this, I was quite surprised to learn that our 13-year-old Eric isn't always truthful online. Take, for example, when he signed up for MySpace.com. As stated in the previous chapter, MySpace is a popular hangout for teens online. It allows teens to create their own digital neighborhoods, where kids like Eric feel at home, can be creative, meet their friends, and meet new friends. For Eric, like many teens, his digital neighborhood is an important part of his social life. So, when MySpace informed him at signup that to share your profile with the world you have to be at least 16, Eric did what many other digital teens have done before and since. He lied. It really bothered me that Eric said he was 19 instead of 13, or even 16. That's a big gap that opens the door to a much older crowd with much older conversations and expectations.

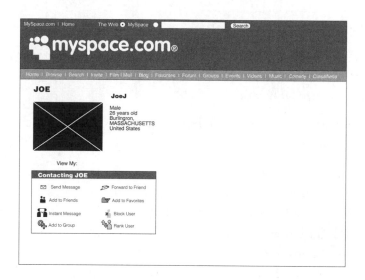

Was I upset that Eric posted to MySpace? No, but I was upset that he lied about his age in such a big way. In my opinion, MySpace.com is one of the coolest sites for teens to create their own digital neighborhood. I wish that places like it had existed when I was his age. My editor, whose own teens prefer to hang out at Xanga, feels the same. Still, I was a little put off by the deception some teens commit to join. It also made me wonder how many other teens had "virtually" adjusted their birth dates to fit in. And, more disturbingly, how many of those young adults weren't really young at all. That's something to consider heavily when you're talking to other members in your favorite digital neighborhood. If your own birth date isn't quite what you claimed, what makes you think that anyone else's is? Maybe that other 19-year-old is really 50 years old. That's gotta creep you out.

I know many adults who think MySpace is a bad space to be. I understand their concerns, and you should to. Here are a few tips for you to remember when creating your digital neighborhood and talking to, well, some of those other teens:

- **Don't bully other teens on MySpace, or anywhere else online.**

  One teen at Hill Middle School, in Novato, California, had to transfer to another school because of other classmates who put up a hate website on MySpace that specifically targeted this teen in a bad way. I hope MySpace bans teens forever from the site when they post hate material about another teen. Don't bully other kids online.

- **Don't give out physical information.**

  Your true physical location is your own safety zone. Don't ever give that away, and try to stay away from telling people what school you go to if you are not really sure who they are.

- **Don't meet people F2F without telling your parents about the meeting, and don't ever go alone.**

  Online crimes are real. And the creeps are out there. If you hang out online you are sure to meet a creep and know it, but some creeps disguise themselves all too well. Be careful. Don't ever meet someone in person who you met online and don't know who they really are. If someone you met online wants to meet you in person, get your parents involved and let them know. Don't ever meet someone F2F if you don't know who they really are.

- **Be careful about what age group you hang out with online.**

  If you are 16 and say you are 25, you are going to meet a lot of older people who wish they were 16. Try to get involved with people who are you own age. You will be 25 before you know it. Enjoy being 16 and meet other people your age. Don't ever assume the person you are talking with online is really the age they say they are.

6.3 Chatting Online—Zero Fear

Most teenagers have no fear when it comes to the Internet. That's a good thing. Being afraid of the Internet would be like being afraid to walk to school, to the mall, or to a friend's house. You can't live in fear. At the same time, however, you need to be aware of your surroundings, protect yourself, and make the right choices in life. You must have the same awareness and make the right choices when you go online.

6.3.1 Instant Messenger

Instant Messenger is certainly one of the most popular tools in my house. We even IM each other when it's time for dinner. Depending on the group I work with, IM is one of the easiest ways to communicate, given how busy people are. Email used to be the simple online form of communication, but IM is much faster if someone is not connected to his or her email program. More telling, I'm NOT the only one in my house using IM. While I might work online, my teenagers seem to LIVE online. As do their friends. Not surprisingly, an AOL study in 2004 found that 90% of teens used Instant Messenger.

> ### IM Often?
>
> By 2004, 7 billion instant messages were being sent DAILY among 250 million IM users!

It makes sense that IM is taking off like crazy. Because you create your buddy list and can block people who are not on the list, you typically are not communicating with strangers. It's like having a private phone with preset Caller ID. You always know who you're talking to before you answer. Or do you? Knowing who you're speaking to is crucial for your own protection.[1]

Given the ease that teens have in opening up emotionally online, it's essential that you really know who you're speaking with. You're probably thinking, but I *know* who's on MY buddy list. These are friends, not strangers! Are you sure? Because of the automatic logon feature, it's incredibly easy to steal IM accounts. You could be speaking to your best friend. Or, your best friend could have unwittingly left logon information at that last Internet cafe that she visited. Are you talking to a classmate? Or someone who happened to walk into the library right after one? For your own safety, you should set a code word with your favorite IM buddies. This way you can ask for the code word if you have any doubt about who it is you're really speaking to.

In the worst case, you may find yourself speaking with someone who's really making you uncomfortable. If you think the person you are communicating with is a pedophile or that person is communicating inappropriately and you aren't sure what to do, keep a record of the date and time of the message, and copy the message into a text file. Keep that record to discuss with your parents. It may be something that your parents feel you need to report to the police.

---

1. Teens are often more comfortable discussing things online than in person. A 2001 study by the Pew Internet & American Life Project group found that over a third of teens had used IM to write things they wouldn't have said in person.

> ### Saving Instant Messages for Later
>
> Most messaging software provides an option to save your conversation for later. In Windows Messenger, simply click **File, Save As...** and assign a name to the created rich text file (*.rtf).

In addition to being careful who you talk to, you should also be careful about what you say when you're chatting online. When 16-year-old Celia received a message from an online friend that contained threats against his schoolmates, she didn't just log off. She printed out the message and took it to the police. The 17-year-old chatter found his comments made public and himself under arrest.

In that particular case, the arrest seemed more than justified. When police searched the chatter's home, they found weapons and disturbing Nazi paraphernalia. More often, it's the case that teens just rant, making silly threats they never intended to carry through. Still, making threats online, even if you don't really mean it, is just as dangerous as sending written threats in the mail. It's also every bit as illegal.

6.3.2 Chat Rooms

Because chat rooms allow members, who are virtual strangers at first, to talk repeatedly and really get to know each other, they pose a special risk to teen users. Sexual predators often spend time in chat rooms to establish friendships with teenagers. They try to strengthen relationships by being friendly and sympathetic, and sometimes by offering gifts. Eventually, those gifts come with an illicit price.[2]

So, how serious is the problem of sexual predators in chat rooms? That depends on who you ask. In October of 2003, Microsoft shut down unsupervised Internet chat rooms in 28 countries, including much of Europe, Africa, Asia, Latin America, and the Middle East. They claimed that the chat rooms "had become a haven for peddlers of junk e-mail and sex predators." The American chat rooms were kept alive, but access was restricted to MSN subscribers—people for whom Microsoft had identification and billing information. Other online forum providers found Microsoft's action serious overkill. Critics also claimed Microsoft's move had as much to do with cutting financial losses as it did with cleaning up the Internet. Still, even if only a handful of predators were out there, that's definitely a handful too many.

---

2. In 2003, some reports claimed that nearly 20% of children were propositioned—nearly three of four of those online. Pedophiles rely on the anonymity of cyberspace as well as the naiveté of younger web surfers.

Luckily, most predators use a pretty standard approach. If you know how these creeps operate, you can avoid them. Furthermore, if you run into problems, you can report them.

In addition to general creeps and perverts, the Internet is also home to a very small but scary number of people who've been dubbed cyberstalkers.

Cyberstalker A predator who uses the Internet (via chat rooms, IM, or email) to harass his victim.

If you know how these creeps operate, you can avoid them.

Cyberstalking is a high-tech form of general stalking. In cyberstalking, the stalker uses online forums such as chat, Instant Messenger, and email to harass his victim. Stalking is more common than you actually think. Some experts claim that up to 5% of adults will be stalked at some point in their lifetime. With cyberstalking, the danger isn't always what the predator says TO you, it's also what the predator says ABOUT you. In recent cases, cyberstalkers have posted personal information (including address and phone number) to public forums along with malicious lies intended to damage the victim's reputation. False claims of drug use and promiscuity are common. Even ignoring the libel issue (slander is spoken), just being repeatedly contacted and harassed by someone you don't want to talk to is disturbing enough.

If you feel you are being stalked, it's important to report it to the police. Keep in mind that this applies to actual stalking. There are real differences between someone who is trying to engage you in bizarre conversation and someone who is stalking and threatening you. You can simply disengage from people who are taking dirty or stupid. Someone who is stalking or threatening you, on the other hand, *needs* to be reported to law enforcement officers. You know the difference.

Got a Creep to Report?

The FBI wants to know. Seriously!

To locate an FBI field office near you, go to www.fbi.gov/contrac/fo/fo.htm.

Don't be afraid to report bad things. The FBI takes online abuse seriously, given the dangers and the reality of the threat. Access to chat rooms typically requires an account, so law enforcement has the authority to track back from the account to the person behind that account.

6.4 Internet Monitoring

Your parents may or may not be concerned about your online acquaintances. If they're not, it's probably because they simply don't realize how connected you are. A lot of parents seem to overlook the fact that home computers are far from the only access children have to the Internet. A few years ago, Internet access was quite limited. Today, teens can choose between home PCs, friends' computers, school labs, libraries, and Internet cafes. I've stayed recently at campgrounds that graciously provided online access to visiting campers. As Lawrence Magid of the National Center for Missing and Exploited Children so accurately noted, "...children don't have to be in the company of responsible adults to use the Internet."

All Eyes on You?

If you're already concerned that your parents might be monitoring and you have opted to use a friend's home computer instead, you may want to consider that *his* parents might be monitoring as well.

If your parents are concerned, they may have installed Internet monitoring software on your home computer. Not *your* parents? Don't be so sure. A 2005 study found that 54% of Internet families used monitoring software. And they really did use it, not just install it. While only a third of teens thought their parents were actually checking where they'd been and what they'd done online, 62% of parents reported doing just that. With a 54% usage rate, the odds are about 50/50 that your parents have Internet monitoring software configured on your home system to keep a close eye on what you are doing online.

Experts are split on whether this is really the most effective way to keep teens online on the right path. One of the problems with software monitoring or keyboard loggers is teens often bypass these controls by using friends' computers, thus bypassing their parent's controls if they really want to.

One method that teens often use to circumvent parental monitoring is collecting **throwaway email accounts**. These are free web-based email accounts, unconnected to your Internet Service Provider, and accessible from any computer with Internet access. Of course, teens aren't the only ones using throwaway accounts. As early as 2001, Microsoft's Hotmail web-based email service had surpassed 100 million accounts. Granted, a good number of those accounts may have been dormant (opened by users who then forgot their passwords or simply never bothered to use the accounts). Still, the number of actual users for freebie accounts is pretty substantial.[3]

Throwaway Email Account A free web-based email account you can access from anywhere and that isn't tied to your Internet Service Provider (ISP).

Another reason people use throwaway accounts is to keep spam away from their "real" email. A number of free Internet services require that you provide a valid email address. However, Outlook now comes with Junk filters that help identify spam. These filters are easy to use and updated by Microsoft.

Using throwaway accounts to avoid spam or check email from summer camp can be useful. That's not true about using throwaway accounts to avoid Internet monitoring. Obviously, it's easy to create accounts on friends' systems and have throwaway accounts on the Internet so your parents don't monitor you. But if you're going around the controls in your home to get to the Internet, you need to ask yourself some tough questions about why you are doing that in the first place.

Communicating over the Internet is not secure. That racy email you deleted from your Sent folder could live on sitting on your email provider's web server for years after you've forgotten what you said or why you said it. Even web pages that have been deleted eons ago still exist on backup tapes and search engine archives. Electronic data never really goes away. It just becomes a little bit harder to find. For this reason, you should NEVER type anything in email, send an instant message,

---

3. According to the Nielsen Net/Ratings, April 2004 alone saw nearly 40 million people actually using Yahoo! Mail and nearly another 35 million at Hotmail.

or transmit a picture over the Internet that you wouldn't want your mother to see. Truthfully, you shouldn't say or post anything online that you wouldn't mind seeing on the front page of the *Wall Street Journal* or the *National Enquirer!*

If you've become that entrenched in your online identity that you're willing to do or say things that you'd never do in person, you need to think about who and what you're becoming. Maybe it is time for you to put the keyboard down for a while and focus on what is important in your life—your grades, your family, friendships that count, and your future.

6.5 Piracy on the Information Superhighway

If you think that the age of piracy ended shortly after the age of chivalry, think again. Just ask the Recording Industry Association of America. On their website, RIAA points out that "Today's pirates operate not on the high seas but on the Internet, in illegal CD factories, distribution centers, and on the street." And the major steals lately seem concentrated on the Internet.

6.5.1 Are You a Pirate?

Pirates don't always manufacture thousands of fake CDs in third-world countries to dump on unsuspecting buyers back home. Sometimes, they download one song or one movie at a time for their own use. There's a public perception that making copies for yourself that you don't plan to sell doesn't really make you a pirate. But that's not how the entertainment industry sees it. If you're downloading copyright-protected songs or videos online, you may very well be a pirate. If you're using that new DVD burner to copy all your friends' personal video libraries, you're definitely a pirate!

> *If you're downloading copyright-protected songs or videos online, you may very well be a pirate.*

Recently Mark, a 14-year-old from San Francisco, asked me, "Why should I pay for music when I can get it for free?" That's a good question with a complicated answer. Part of this answer is that it's just the right thing to do. It's also the properly legal thing to do. Legal details are a bit complex to explain, so let's start with "right" first.

The Right Stuff

Let's imagine that you and your buddies are starting a new band. It could be heavy metal, pop rock, rap, country western—whatever you are great at. Your guitar player, Jamie, even has a special "in" for you. His father produces music for a living.

Not long after you begin, your garage band takes off. Soon afterwards, Jamie's dad helps you cut your very first commercial CD. This is great! You've accomplished what every grunge band in history merely dreams of—you get a hit song out of the gate and begin to receive royalties. Incredible luck, right? Only partly. You also put a TON of work into that success. You and your band practiced six days a week, not just one. You worked your guts out nailing down the right lyrics.

Now imagine that your CD is showing up on all those "free" music download sites. Everybody's listening to your work, but nobody's actually paying you. Now how would you feel? It wouldn't be right, would it?

The Legal Stuff

If the music being stolen from the Net were personally yours, you'd probably be pretty upset. You might even begin prosecuting anyone you caught in the act of stealing it. This pretty much sums up how the music industry feels. They've gotten very tired of seeing their profits downloaded away and they've begun to demand that courts hold ANYONE they catch accountable.

The key word here is ANYONE. Obviously, the music industry sets their sights highest on shutting down the major pirating factories abroad. But they're also going after the little guys right here. And those little guys include teenagers.

6.5.2 Are You Putting Your Parents at Risk?

I used to hate buying an entire CD when all I wanted was one song. It is great to be able to purchase a single song instead of a whole CD, or to be able to download just a few songs and store them on an iPod. It probably seems even better when those few songs are "free."

In real life, however, few things are truly free. Downloading music without paying for it is not one of those things. It is stealing from the recording artists. That's the law, and the Recording Industry Association of America (RIAA) and the Motion Picture Association of America (MPAA) are losing patience with the practice.

In the past, people thought that it was only a crime if you made a copy you were planning to sell. With easy downloads, however, the practice of making personal copies has become so common that it's costing the entertainment industry a fortune. For years now, music sales and profits have either dropped or remained flat—an effect many blame on the pervasiveness of online piracy.

To project jobs, and profits, the big boys in the entertainment industry have started going after the little guys in a big way. One of their first targets was 12-year-old Brianna LaHara. Living in a Housing Authority apartment, Brianna hardly represented a major piracy ring. Like most young teens, she downloaded music only for her own use.

The press of course had a field day with the lawsuit, as did Congress. During later Senate Judiciary Hearings addressing music piracy, one senator sarcastically asked the RIAA president, "Are you headed to junior high schools to round up the usual suspects?" In the end, though, the RIAA had the law on its side because downloading or simply making copyrighted material available for download without the permission of the owner is illegal. While she avoided the major fines she could have faced, Brianna's exploits cost her a $2,000 fine. Just imagine how many legal CDs she could have bought with that money.

While pirating music may seem thrifty in the short term, it can cost you and your parents big money if you're caught. While the settlements in early cases (circa 2003) have ranged from $2,000 to $7,500, American copyright law actually allows

The Most Stolen Items

The "hottest" products being illegally downloaded from the Net:

- Music
- Movies
- Software applications

for damages of up to $150,000 per song. Before you download your next mix, you might consider whether your "free" CD is worth risking your parents' house. The RIAA and MPAA are actively looking for abusers. Don't give them an easy target.

Even if you're not putting your parents at legal risk by your downloading activities, you could still be putting their data at risk. As you'll remember from Chapter 3, "Data Grabbers and Dumpers," downloading "freebies" from peer-to-peer networks also brings a major risk of downloading spyware, adware, and Trojan horses. Why risk the integrity of your computer or the money your parents have stashed in your college fund? It's not worth it.

Chapter 7

Phishing for Dollars

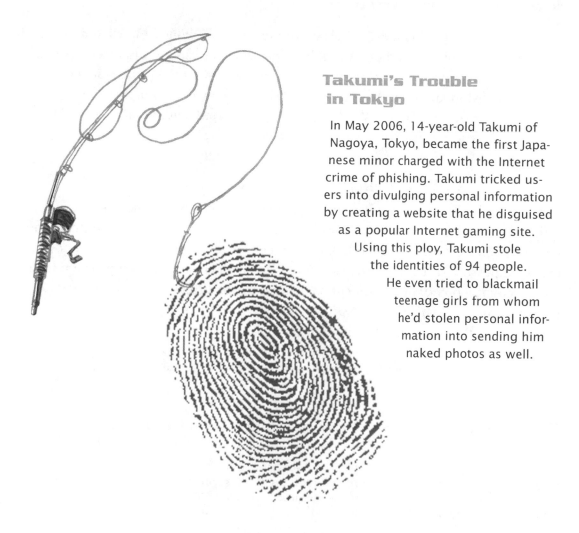

Takumi's Trouble in Tokyo

In May 2006, 14-year-old Takumi of Nagoya, Tokyo, became the first Japanese minor charged with the Internet crime of phishing. Takumi tricked users into divulging personal information by creating a website that he disguised as a popular Internet gaming site. Using this ploy, Takumi stole the identities of 94 people. He even tried to blackmail teenage girls from whom he'd stolen personal information into sending him naked photos as well.

Obviously Takumi wasn't the brightest fisherman in the sea. He was also far from the first teen to fall prey to his own bait. A U.S. teen with more of a penchant for cash than photos was caught on his own phishing line in July 2003. Seventeen-year-old Michael used spam emails and a fake AOL web page to trick people out of credit card information that he used to steal thousands of dollars. While his plan was incredibly ill-advised, Michael himself was incredibly lucky when prosecutors agreed to a return of the stolen funds instead of serious jail time. Today, it's very unlikely a deal that generous would be offered. Since 2003, we've learned just how devastating and costly Internet crime can be.

Given the antics of Takumi and Michael, you're probably wondering what an experienced adult criminal could do! You'll be surprised. This chapter discusses phishing scams in detail and provides a pretty good overview of what the professional criminals can do. More importantly, this chapter tells you how to spot a phishing expedition. For their own good, that's a skill you'll want to share with your parents. They may not know just how easy it is to get hooked.

7.1 What Is Phishing?

As I said earlier, **phishing** (pronounced *fishing*) is just what it sounds like—con artists fishing for information. In computer terms, a phishing attack generally begins with a spoofed email. That email pretends to be from a company you know and trust and possibly already do business with. The email claims there's a problem with your account, potentially fraudulent use or charges, or simply asks you to verify your information to help them to protect you. That's actually a nice bit of social engineering—the con artist offering to protect you from security risks.

Phishing   An attempt via email and faked websites to trick users into revealing personal information or financial data.

Here is a good example of a well-known phishing attempt, the PayPal scam:

```
Dear PayPal Customer,

We are currently performing regular maintenance of our security measures. Your account
has been randomly selected for this maintenance, and you will now be taken through a
series of identity verification pages.
```

Protecting the security of your PayPal account is our primary concern, and we apologize for any inconvenience this may cause. Please confirm your account ownership by entering the information in one of the sections below.

Please Visit
https://www.paypal.com/cgi-bin/webscr?cmd=_login-run
and take a moment to confirm your account. To avoid service interruption we require that you confirm your account as soon as possible.
Your account will be updated in our system and you may continue using PayPal services without any interruptions.

If you fail to update your account, it will be flagged with restricted status.

Thank you,
The PayPal Staff
Thanks for using PayPal!

PROTECT YOUR PASSWORD

NEVER give your password to anyone and ONLY log in at
https://www.paypal.com/cgi-bin/webscr?cmd=_login-run
Protect yourself against fraudulent websites by checking the URL/Address bar every time you log in.

If you've used the Internet to buy anything at auction, you're no doubt familiar with PayPal. PayPal is the online service that most people use to pay for items that they purchase on sites such as eBay. While it's not technically a bank, PayPal functions very close to a bank, allowing you to transfer money easily to any other PayPal user by simply sending an email message. Those types of transfers are possible because when you (or your parents) set up your PayPal account, they linked that PayPal account to an actual bank account or to a credit card.

Online shoppers like PayPal because it feels safer than handing out credit card numbers to perfect strangers. So what's the problem? In recent years, PayPal has also become a major target for hackers and phishers. And it's not alone. While we've talked about denial-of-service (DoS) attacks and worms aimed at taking out commercial websites, the biggest problem to hit most of the big online players—PayPal, eBay, Amazon, etc.—in recent years really hasn't been security issues on their sites. The biggest problem has been phishers scamming financial details from their customers.

If you've used PayPal to purchase an auction item, you've probably already been hit by this scam. Even if you don't have a PayPal account, you've probably been hit by this scam. That's because phishers are a lot like spammers. They go for quantity, not quality. Since PayPal has over 78 million users operating in 56 countries, chances are that a good percentage of email addresses that phishers spam are going to actually be PayPal customers. Do they bother to check? No. This may also explain why your parents may have gotten requests to "update information" for credit cards they don't actually hold. Phishers, like spammers, are just playing the numbers. If even a small percentage of consumers take the bait, they clean up.

You'll notice that our sample PayPal scam email asks you to visit a specific web page, https://www.paypal.com/cgi-bin/webscr?cmd=_login-run. This is a common component of any phishing attempt, the embedded link. At some point, the phishing emails all ask you to click the link provided to log into your account and update or verify your account information. The problem, of course, is that the link doesn't take you to your actual account. Instead, it routes you to a fake screen—often a series of fake screens—that have the same look and feel as the actual company.

If you follow the link, anything that you type from that point forward is sent directly to the con artist responsible for the phishing attempt. If you enter a user name and password, you're giving that con artist everything he needs to impersonate you on that site. When the phishing target is a bank or bank-like account such as PayPal, you're giving the criminal all the details he needs to literally empty your accounts. If you enter credit card information, you should expect some unexpected charges to follow shortly. You may even be providing all the data that crook needs to successfully steal your identity. If that happens, new charges on your accounts may be the least of your worries. A savvy thief could open countless NEW charge cards in your

> *In recent years, PayPal has become a major target for hackers and phishers.*

name, littering your credit report with unpaid accounts that could destroy your financial history almost before you've had a chance to even acquire one.

Keep in mind that email isn't the only method used for phishing. The basic phishing scam actually predates computers by many decades. The big change here is that computers make it easier for the con artists to hide. Because emails are often created using spoofed addresses and fake routing information, they are difficult to trace.

7.1.1 How Common Are Phishing Attacks?

Incredibly common. In June 2005, anti-spam service Postini alone claimed to have stopped 16,667,444 phishing attempts from being delivered to its clients. While this sounds high, it's probably not. All experts reported major jumps in phishing in 2005, and that was starting from a baseline of *over 18 million* phishing expeditions in 2004. Why so common? From the phisher's point of view, the tactic works. Early figures (circa 2003 and 2004) found nearly one in five users were taken in by the spoofed emails and websites. While people are becoming a bit more savvy (or perhaps just apprehensive), far too many still fall for the phishing lures.

7.1.2 Who Gets "Phished"?

While it's individual customers who are hooked, the victims of phishing also include all those companies whose customers lose confidence, and in some cases, even stop using their online services. These include all types and sizes of businesses, but the major victims are online services and financial groups.

Banks

For obvious reasons, banks are MAJOR targets in phishing scams. In 2004, the California-based Anti-Phishing Working Group claimed that phishing attacks had been launched against MOST major banks in the United States, Australia, and Great Britain. Even scams that fail cost banks a small fortune in the costs required to cancel accounts and reissue new credit cards. As a good-faith gesture, customers receive new cards free of charge. Eventually though, we all pay those fees in higher credit card costs.

Online Companies

Because online businesses often depend on email as their only method of communicating with customers, these firms are hit hardest by phishing scams. Because they represent three of the largest online firms, eBay, PayPal, and Amazon are targeted often.

Almost ANY Group or Organization with an Online Presence

Some of the scammers are really fearless. In January 2005, one especially gutsy scammer sent a phishing email that purported to come from the Federal Deposit Insurance Corporation (FDIC), the government agency that regulates banks and provides customers with insurance protection in the event that a bank ever went out of business. Neither the FDIC nor the FBI (which the FDIC called in ASAP) was impressed.

```
Joint Release     FEDERAL DEPOSIT INSURANCE CORPORATION
FEDERAL BUREAU OF INVESTIGATION
-----------------------------------------------------------

FOR IMMEDIATE RELEASE
FDIC-PR-6-2004  January 23, 2004

FDIC And FBI Investigating Fraudulent Emails

At approximately 12:00 p.m. (EST) on January 23, 2004, FDIC Consumer Call Centers
in Kansas City, Missouri, and Washington, D.C., began receiving a large number of
complaints by consumers who received an email that has the appearance of being sent from
the FDIC. The email informs the recipient that Department of Homeland Security Director
Tom Ridge has advised the FDIC to suspend all deposit insurance on the recipient's bank
account due to suspected violations of the USA PATRIOT Act. The email further indicates
that deposit insurance will be suspended until personal identity, including bank account
information, can be verified.

This email was not sent by the FDIC and is a fraudulent attempt to obtain personal
information from consumers. Financial institutions and consumers should NOT access
the link provided within the body of the email and should NOT under any circumstances
provide any personal information through this media.
```

Probably You

Given that even Uncle Sam is being phished, there's little reason to believe that you won't land on the scammers' lists in the near future. Are you one of the 73 million users who've been to MySpace? If so, you may have already been phished and not know it. In early June 2006, a spoofed site phishing for MySpace.com logins was discovered and removed in California. An *especially* sly attack, the hacker used IM to send invites to view photos that appeared to come from one of the target victim's online "friends." If the target bit and used the embedded link provided, he was really entering his logon details to a fraudulent site that captured the logon information while passing it on and using those details to really log him onto MySpace. Since the time lag was minimal and the user really ended up at MySpace, chances are good that none of the victims ever knew their information had been stolen.

7.2 How to Recognize a Phishing Trip

No one likes being taken for a ride. To avoid being pulled into an unwanted phishing trip, you need to understand two things. First, you need to realize just how good and how convincing the fakes are. Second, you need to know exactly what to look for to spot the phonies.

7.2.1 How Good Are the Fakes?

The fake screens can be *very* convincing. Notice the email shown in **Figure 7.1**, another phishing attempt to trick PayPal users into revealing their user names and passwords.

The spoofed screen is pretty convincing, isn't it? Notice the ads for PayPal Visa and eBay. Now compare this to an ACTUAL PayPal screen shown in **Figure 7.2** (in this case, appropriately, the Help screen to tell users how to recognize fake PayPal emails and avoid being taken in).

Overall, the phishers did an excellent job here. You'll note that the PayPal logo is virtually identical, as is the style and color scheme of the screen layout. The spoofed logo is missing the registered trademark symbol (®) but is otherwise an excellent copy. There's a *very* slight difference in the saturation level of the deep blue bar running under the PayPal logo—the fake bar is just a smidge less blue than the original. But again, this is close enough that you'd need to lay them side by side to notice any distinction, and even then, it won't be obvious to most users. The end result? The fake screen has the exact look and feel of the actual screen.

Figure 7.1

Spoofed PayPal screen included in phishing attempt

Figure 7.2

Actual PayPal screen

The spoofed messages themselves are so convincing that up to 20% of recipients respond to them. That's a lot of people putting a lot of personal and financial data at risk.

7.2.2 How Can I Recognize a Phishing Scam?

In *Harry Potter and the Prisoner of Azkaban*, J. K. Rowling introduces a wonderful device called a *sneakoscope*. While tuned to look mostly for dark magic, the basic idea is that the sneakoscope goes off when it encounters persons or things basically up to no good. Products are being developed to spot this fraudulent activity, because it's easy for humans to miss some of the simple fraud attacks.

Once you know what to look for, it becomes easier to spot the spoofs. Quite a number of features tend to give away the fakes. These include the use of generic names, a logo that doesn't quite match, poor grammar, verification requests, and masked web addresses. The appearance of any ONE of these items should set off your internal sneakoscope.

Do I Know You?

As Shakespeare put it so eloquently in *Romeo and Juliet*, "What's in a name? That which we call a rose by any other name would smell as sweet." That may be well and good for flowers, but via email what the message sender calls you lets you know, in large part, who it is you're really talking to.

With phishing scams, the spammed email nearly always begins with some euphemism filling the space where your name should really be:

- Dear Online Service user:
- Dear Bank customer:
- Dear Credit Card account holder:
- Dear Personal Club member:

Sometimes, the scammers try to make this less obvious by omitting "Dear" and beginning with a salutation that doesn't normally require a name:

- Greetings!
- Welcome!
- Warning!
- Security alert!

With very few exceptions, any valid email you receive requesting additional information is going to come from a company that knows you as well as you know it. Your bank actually knows your first and last name. So does the company that issued your parents' credit card. To protect your identity as well as their finances, never provide any information in response to an email that doesn't identify you by name.

Because of the high incidence of phishing attempts, many companies are now adding names to what would once have been basic form letters. For example, this eBay customer knew that the email actually came from eBay because it also contained the following line above the form letter salutation:

```
eBay sent this message to Denise L Weldon-Siviy(compulsive_reader).
Your registered name is included to show this message originated from eBay.
```

Using Goodly Grammar

If your mother's like mine, she probably reminded you a thousand times to pay attention to your grammar to avoid sounding shallow or ignorant.

For reasons that almost defy comprehension, given the easy availability and use of grammar checkers, most phishing letters contain bad, if not downright awful, grammar. Consider this extract from a phishing email sent to Amazon users:

```
Greetings!
Due to simultaneous fraud attempts we received. We regularly update and verify our
customers. During a random review by our department there was a problem in your account
that we could not verify your account information. Either your information has changed
or it is incomplete.
```

What's wrong with this paragraph? For starters, the first sentence is a fragment. "Due to simultaneous fraud attempts we received." While that first sentence stops short, the third sentence continues too far and becomes a run-on. The fact that this scam was directed at Amazon was a nice touch of irony. Do you really think that the world's largest bookseller is incapable of writing a coherent sentence? This is a good example of why you need to pay attention in your English class!

The Devil Is in the Details

A near constant in phishing attempts is the request that you "verify your account" or "confirm your account information." In essence, the con artist wants you to provide all the details that would allow him to use your account.

Because of privacy regulations, security issues, and plain-old common sense, legitimate companies will NEVER ask you to verify the following types of information:

- Pin numbers
- Passwords
- Bank account numbers
- Credit card numbers

Know Where You're Going

Another dead giveaway that you're being directed to a fake website is mismatched URLs.

URL (Uniform Resource Locator)   The word-like address used to locate a specific web page on the Internet.

In the case of phishing attempts that try to trick you into going to a fake website, you'll find that the URL printed in the email message won't match the URL displayed when you mouse over the link. In some cases, what you'll see in the mouse-over is a series of numbers corresponding to an IP address. This is no doubt a real Internet address, but most certainly NOT the one you thought you were being sent to.

In other cases, you'll see a URL that looks very close to what you'd expect. Close, but not quite close enough. Often, the fake URL will contain extra letters or words that aren't part of the real web address. For example, in the phishing letter shown at the front of this chapter, mousing over the included link displays what's shown in **Figure 7.3**.

Please Visit

https://www.paypal.com/cgi-bin/webscr?cmd=_login-run

http://www.paypal-transactions.com/cgi-bin/webscr-cmd-_login-run

Figure 7.3
Fake PayPal URL

While this looks official, the URL www.paypal-transactions.com is NOT the same as www.paypal.com. In all likelihood, the errant address isn't even owned by PayPal.

Another common technique is to omit or reverse a few letters. In this way, www.amazon.com becomes www.amzaon.com or www.amzon.com. The addresses are so close that people just skimming—and not really looking for tricks—are easily fooled. You may have seen several web addresses like this without even realizing they were fakes. Research conducted by reading specialists has found that our minds automatically fill in missing letters and words without most readers even noticing. Like so many parts of phishing, this is another practical application of social engineering.

7.3 Don't Let the Phishers Hook You

Legitimate banks and e-commerce sites never send emails requesting account numbers, passwords, social security numbers, or other personal information. The problem, however, is that the emails phishers send requesting this information look so real that many people have been tricked into giving the phishers what they are looking for. Phishers are becoming clever and are using spam and malicious code to increase the likelihood of getting your personal information. They will continue to do so ruthlessly. If a company with which you are doing business sends you or your parents an email asking you to update your account, don't.

Don't ever update or provide a bank account number, login information, social security number, or any other kind of personal information, no matter how official the site looks. Your parents might not be aware of this type of fraud, so educate them and make sure they don't get hooked by phishers.

Chapter 8

Taming the Cookie Monster

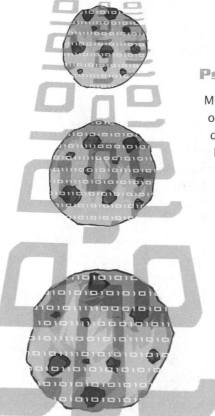

Psychic Sites

Mike spent a lot of time surfing PC gaming sites on the Internet. Still, he was a little put off one day when visiting an old gaming site he hadn't been to in 5 or 6 months. Just connecting to the site, without logging in or providing any information, he was greeted as a welcomed old friend:

Welcome Back Mike of Bendersville!

While the goal was to bring Mike figuratively back into the fold, the effect was that it actually creeped him out. Mike began to wonder exactly how the gaming site knew *who* he was. He began to wonder if he'd fallen victim to that spyware he'd been hearing so much about...

While it's possible that Mike had fallen victim to spyware, the link to those details that creeped him out was probably stored on his own computer, sitting in plain sight in his Cookies folder.

8.1 What Exactly Is a Cookie?

Contrary to popular belief, a **cookie** is not a program. It doesn't DO anything per se. It's simply a text file that stores information. Cookies land on your computer almost continuously every time you surf the Net. Those cookies are then accessed, over and over again, every time you revisit websites. Accepting cookies, whether you realize it or not, is part of using most websites on the Internet.

Cookie A text file written to your hard drive by a website that you visit. A website can use a cookie to recognize you, and sometimes remember custom settings, when you visit that site again in the future.

In general terms, a cookie is a small text file that usually stores a single item—a name/value pair. In most cases, the "name" is a conglomeration of the website name and the user ID you've selected (or have been assigned) for the site you're visiting. The "value" is a unique numeric value that the site has assigned to that name. Together, the name/value pair uniquely identifies you every time that you visit that website from the same computer.

If you're curious, you can look at your cookies (and, *yes*, you most definitely have them!). Assuming that you're using a Windows-based system, do the following:

1. Click **Start.**
2. Click **My Computer.**
3. Double-click the **Local Disk (C:)** icon.
4. Double-click the **Documents and Settings** folder.
5. Double-click the folder name that identifies you as a user. (The folder name in this example is **Denise.**)
6. Double-click the **Cookies** folder.

You should see a listing of cookies on your hard drive.

This gives you a quick view of all the cookies on your hard drive. You'll notice that our example is a pretty short list. That's because this is only 1 hour's worth of cookies! Unless you've also killed your cookie files recently, you're more likely to see at least one or two HUNDRED cookies on your own machine.

Regardless of how many cookies you have, each cookie is usually a single name/ value pair. To actually look at one, double-click on the cookie name. **Figure 8.1** shows an example of a MySpace cookie.

Figure 8.1

Example of MySpace cookie

As you can see, cookies also really aren't very informational to look at. They are, however, a very important thing to know about.

8.2 Are Cookies Good for Me?

For years, the only thing harder to find in my living room than the TV remote was the program listing from the Sunday paper. Desperate to know our options without spending half the show time flipping through the channels, we were resigned to painfully trying to watch those tiny rows scrolling across the *TV Guide* channel.

While that seems an ideal solution, it really didn't work out that way. Regardless of what time we tuned into the channel listings, the list was invariably just beginning the endless trip through digital channels we don't get, premium channels we don't subscribe to, and pay-per-view options we weren't willing to pay for. By the time the broadcast channels and basic cable options rolled around, we'd naturally gotten distracted by the interview or "making of" documentary broadcast on the top half of the screen. You guessed it—we missed what we were looking for and had to cycle through again. Needless to say, we were thrilled to discover the *TV Guide* website. One 30-second detour from the TV set to the living room computer only 10 feet away and we knew what was on *before* it was half over!

So how does this relate to cookies? Like most websites, the *TV Guide* website operates using cookies. In fact, *TV Guide* places three cookies on your hard drive the first time you use it. While it's nearly impossible to tell what these cookies are for by just viewing them, they seem to perform three basic functions. From what I can tell, these cookies (1) identify your machine as a regular viewer (to keep track of how often you return), (2) remember your ZIP Code so you're shown the TV listings for your time zone, and (3) keep track of your cable company or satellite provider to give you an accurate listing of the shows that are available to you. Without those cookies, it would be impossible for *TV Guide* to serve its purpose—to give you a customized listing of the shows you're actually able to watch.

> *Cookies allow the websites you visit to keep track of you.*

Of course, this is only one of MANY "good" uses of cookies. Cookies allow websites to customize what they show you to best meet your needs. Cookies also allow you to customize your view of websites. Or, more specifically, they allow the website to *remember* your customizations. Otherwise, you'd need to "customize" each site every time that you visited. That would hardly be convenient. Cookies also allow you to set convenient options, such as one-click shopping and checkout on commercial sites, and the ability for sites to "remember you," thus removing the need for you to enter your user name and password every time you visit.

But like wizards, not all cookies are good. Cookies also allow the websites you visit to keep track of you. They can record how often you visit, and which pages you use on their sites. The potential for Big Brother–style oversight by cookies and their evil cousins, web bugs, makes a lot of web users VERY uncomfortable.

8.3 Who Eats All Those Cookies?

If you're wondering how you can tell whether a website is using cookies, often you can't. However, there is one dead giveaway. If a website greets you by name when you access it, there is no doubt whatsoever that they're using cookies. Otherwise, how could they know your name?

8.3.1 Primary Cookies

In general, there are two kinds of sites that "eat" cookies: primary websites and third-party sites. The primary website is the site you in fact went to visit. If you've visited MySpace.com and ended up with a MySpace cookie on your hard drive, MySpace is the primary website. That's hardly surprising. Often, you want and/or need the primary site to store a cookie to allow you to best use that site.

8.3.2 Third-Party Cookies

Third-party cookies are placed on your machine from a website you never visited. We talked earlier about web bugs, also called web beacons and transparent GIFs. A web bug is a graphic so small you can't see it that is included on a web page. When you visit that web page, the "invisible" graphic is downloaded from a different web page. That "different" web page is called a *third-party site* because it's not the primary (first-party) site that you visited, and it's not you (the second party). That makes it the third party.

Third-Party Cookie A cookie placed on your machine from a website you DIDN'T actually visit.

Technically, viewing a web page that contains a web bug downloading from a third-party site has the same effect as loading that third-party web page into your web browser. So, any cookies that would be sent by that third-party site also land on your computer. Using these invisible graphics, advertisers and **data pharmers** (people who "farm" the Internet for information about its users) can place cookies on your computer without you ever realizing that you've visited their websites. Even worse, when those third-party cookies are linked to web bugs sent via email, the pharmers can match your email address up with any details stored on the cookie. Scan enough cookies, add the email address, and it's not long before the data pharmers can actually identify YOU, not just the cookie.

Data Pharmer   Someone who "farms" the Internet, growing collections (databases) of information about Internet users.

8.4 What If I Don't Want to Share?

If you're concerned about the cookies you may have accumulated on your hard drive, you can always decide to remove them. Doing so will help to keep advertisers from tracking you. For many web users, that's a comforting thought. Keep in mind, of course, that if you delete your cookies you may need to recustomize many of the websites you visit.

8.4.1 Emptying Your Cookies Folder

If you had a look at your own Cookies folder earlier in this chapter (as you probably did!), you may have decided to remove a few of those cookies. Maybe even all of them. You can remove cookies from your machine in several ways.

Using Explorer

To delete cookies using Internet Explorer, do the following:

1. Within Internet Explorer, click **Tools** on the menu bar.

2. Click on **Internet Options....** This opens the dialog box shown in **Figure 8.2**.

3. Click the button **Delete Cookies**.

This removes ALL the cookies in your Cookies folder. If you'd prefer to remove only some (and leave the cookies from sites you know and trust), you'll want to use My Computer instead.

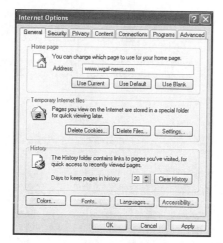

Figure 8.2
Internet Explorer options

Using My Computer

To delete cookies using My Computer, do the following:

1. Click **Start**.

2. Click **My Computer**.

3. Double-click the **Local Disk (C:)** icon.

4. Double-click the **Documents and Settings** folder.

5. Double-click the folder name that identifies you as a user.

6. Double-click the **Cookies** folder.

7. Select the cookies you specifically want to delete. (To kill all of them, use the **Edit, Select All** menu option.)

8. Press the **Delete** key.

9. Click **Yes** to confirm the deletion.

8.4.2 Do All Cookies Live in My Cookies Folder?

No. This is why deleting cookies doesn't always keep sites from recognizing you. Sometimes, you agree to have cookies placed somewhere else on your computer. For example, let's imagine that you check the weather every day, as many people do. When you sign up for custom updates at Weather.com, you actually have the option of storing a cookie outside of your Cookies folder (see **Figure 8.3**).

Figure 8.3
Alternate Cookies folders

As the description explains, this isn't an unreasonable thing to do. In fact, my only problem here (and why I said No to this option) is that they tell you only that they place the cookie in a "different location." They don't actually tell you WHERE they put it. If I ever wanted to get rid of that copied cookie, I'd have no idea where to start since I don't know either the name of the cookie text file or the exact location where they put it. This is like saying, since I know you're likely to forget your locker combination, I'm going to hide a copy of it somewhere in your room. However, I'm not going to tell you where it is. If you want that information back, you need to come to me. I prefer to hold my own information.

What's even more of a problem is that less scrupulous companies may not tell you at all that they're hiding cookie information outside your Cookies folder. This allows them to continue to recognize you and track your visits even if you delete ALL your cookies.

8.4.3 Keeping Cookies Out of the Jar

Usually, cookies don't include personally identifying information about you. However, that doesn't mean that the company that placed the cookies hasn't started a database file on you collecting detailed personal information. And of course, since they know your cookie and use it to identify you when you visit their site, they could easily store that cookie along with that database data. Thus, cookies can be, and often are, used in data pharming operations to collect pretty detailed information about you, who you are, and what you do online. Data pharmers make good monetary (if not moral) livings by collecting and reselling that information.

When you visit a site online, the **privacy policies** of that website should tell you how and if that site collects and shares information about you. Unfortunately, most people don't take time to read these policies.

Privacy Policy The official policy of a commercial website telling you what (if any) information it collects about you and what it does with that information.

If you are using Internet Explorer, there are some simple steps you can take to control how cookies can be set on your PC. In theory, you can even block cookies altogether. Unfortunately, if you do block all cookies—including first-party cookies—you may find that you're unable to use many pages on the Internet. For example, if you choose to Block All Cookies in Internet Explorer, you will soon find that your Yahoo! mail account simply won't work.

Remember also that many cookies are good. They provide added richness and utility to the websites you use most often. So, you really don't want to block all cookies and certainly not all first-party cookies. The trick is to find a happy medium.

Medium—specifically Medium High—really is your desired setting. To set your cookie tolerance to this level, do the following:

1. In Internet Explorer, click **Tools** on the menu bar.

2. Select **Internet Options...** This displays the Internet Options dialog box, shown in **Figure 8.4**.

3. Click on the **Privacy** tab, as shown in **Figure 8.5**.

4. Drag the marker on the left to **Medium High,** as shown in **Figure 8.5**.

5. Click **Apply.**

6. Click **OK.**

This setting provides a reasonable level of privacy without sacrificing the functions that let the Internet serve YOUR needs.

Figure 8.4

Controlling cookies

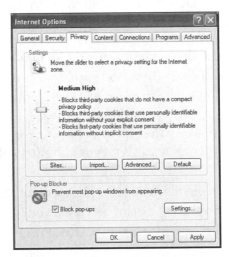

Figure 8.5

Blocking third-party cookies

8.5 Clearing the Crumbs

Like real cookies are good for the taste buds but usually bad for the hips, electronic cookies can also be both good and bad. At first glance, it's hard to see a bad side to an electronic shortcut that allows you to customize your web surfing experience with minimal effort. In their best light, cookies save you time and make your web surfing more comfortable, convenient, and efficient.

At the same time, however, cookies ARE a threat because they collect information about what you do online. They keep track of which websites you visit and how often you visit them. Like any other type of information collection done without your explicit consent, they represent a threat to your privacy.

Cookies can also represent a threat to your identity and your personal information. While cookies themselves don't store passwords or personal information, they identify your computer to websites on which you may very well have entered identifying information. Using cookies associated with web bugs, savvy data pharmers can glue the pieces together—email address, personal information entered online, web surfing habits. The cookie itself may not contain any sensitive data, but it's the map that links the pieces together for the data pharmer.

Chapter 9

Safe Cyber-Shopping

Who Needs the Mall, Anyway?

Meet Frank Wong, a 15-year-old cyber-shopper from Cleveland, Ohio.

Frank began his online commerce experience when he used his mom Sally's credit card to open his Xbox 360 account. A few weeks later, Sally was blown away when Frank asked if he could buy his T-shirts online. The mall simply did not carry the cool shirts that Frank wanted. Buying Frank's T-shirts online saved her a trip to the mall and she has been buying T-shirts, books, and anything else he needs on the Internet ever since. Sally hates the mall.

I NEED SOME NEW SHORTS FROM HOT TOPIC...

Today, Frank still can't remember the combination to his school locker. But he has memorized Sally's Visa number, even the expiration date and verification code! Sally's not all that thrilled about his ability to memorize her credit card information, but she loves shopping online.

This year, Sally will be far from the only mom—or dad—skipping the mall for the convenience of shopping online. **E-commerce** has rapidly become a major part of the American consumer experience. With the right security installed online, shopping can be a great experience.

e-commerce (Electronic commerce)   The business of buying and selling stuff online.

A mere decade ago, online shopping seemed the province of upscale professionals and the technological elite. No more. Today, grandmothers and programmers alike peruse Amazon and eToys for that perfect birthday gift. The ranks of eBay users have also swelled to include a substantial percentage of holiday shoppers.

Still, the teen market still seems to lead the way. By mid-2005, 43% of American teens had purchased one or more items online. For teen girls between 15 and 17, online shoppers now form a majority at 51%.

As online shopping has taken off, the general public has also become more aware of both privacy and security issues. Sending credit card numbers and **e-checks** makes some people a bit paranoid.

e-check   An electronic version of a bank check. Unlike a money order (which is a check-like piece of paper anyone can buy using cash, even if they don't have a checking account), an e-check is tied to a specific bank account just like a real check. It simply exists only electronically, not on paper.

And it should, but within reason. Although online fraud has expanded along with the expansion of e-commerce, online paranoia has expanded even faster. Should you be careful about shipping off your parents' Visa numbers to perfect strangers? Absolutely! Is this really more dangerous than handing their credit card to another teen cashier at the mall? Maybe not.

Obviously, there are real dangers and risks in using those Check Out options on the Internet. But it's important to put those dangers in perspective. In this chapter, we'll examine the real risks of online commerce and talk frankly about how to minimize those dangers while taking advantage of the wonders and freedoms provided by putting the world's malls at the tips of your keyboarding fingers.

9.1 Online Shopping Basics

Total e-commerce sales for 2004 topped $69 billion. If you're wondering who it is that is doing all that online shopping, the answer is pretty much everyone! In the early years of e-commerce, roughly the mid-1990s, the average online shopper was a young, fairly affluent man. Today, that shopper looks much like the average American. Current e-shoppers are middle age, middle income, and (like the population at large) slightly more likely to be female than male. That is, e-shoppers now look pretty much like the shoppers you'd meet in person at your neighborhood mall.

An important development is that online shoppers now fall into nearly every age range and most socioeconomic groups. Obviously, the poorest shoppers account for far fewer online purchases. Of course, they also account for far fewer purchases of any kind. Surprisingly though, the highest sales came from middle-income rather than the most affluent shoppers. Price-conscious netizens are especially pleased with the experience, using search engines and comparison shopping sites to get the most bang from their shopping buck.

The ease of online shopping solutions has also played a major role.

The spread of faster broadband connections has also had an effect on online purchases.[1] No longer forced to wait for detailed photos or websites to download, broadband users account for over two-thirds of online purchases.

Looking for a Better Deal?

Easy comparison shopping is one of many areas where online commerce beats the socks off traditional brick-and-mortar establishments. To compare prices on your upcoming purchases, try one of 2005's top comparison shopping sites:

- Froogle
- NextTag
- PriceGrabber
- Shop.com
- Shopping.com
- Shopzilla
- Yahoo Shopping

---

1. By 2000, a full 40% of Internet users had made at least one purchase online. By 2005, surging gasoline prices also factored in as shoppers made fewer trips to brick-and-mortar establishments and seemed to apply the savings in auto fuel costs to additional online purchases.

These numbers are likely to continue growing. Several studies have found that once a consumer makes a "good" online purchase, she's very likely to make more and more purchase online. And, despite the hype over online scams and identity theft, most online purchases are good.[2]

9.1.1 What Are They Buying?

Mention online buying to an average newbie and you're likely to get a comment about eBay. While the online auction giant is still the place to go for obscure teacups and collectibles of any genre, eBay no longer rules the roost in online sales. By 2005, the top markets included fixed-price offerings by both e-commerce-only sites and online versions of traditional chains.

So what are shoppers buying online? Almost everything:

Electronics and Computer Goods

As you might expect, electronic goods sell briskly online. After all, these are the goods specifically targeted to the most technologically savvy online users.

Clothing

When LL Bean and Land's End began offering online shopping to traditional catalogue customers, they began a trend and they've been joined by Old Navy, Gap, American Eagle, Abercrombie, and so on.

Books

Sales of both new and used books have also surged online. While Amazon leads the pack, a wide variety of challengers (Barnes and Noble, Abe Books, etc.) still follow with strong sales figures. Amazon, of course, sets some pretty astronomical figures to follow. During the 2004 holiday season, Amazon buyers purchased 2.8 million items, setting a rate of 32 online purchases per second. While not all of those purchases were books (Amazon also offers electronics, music, DVDs, etc.), that's still a lot of happy readers!

---

2. Fully 80% of shoppers were completely satisfied with their latest online purchases. One industry analyst, Forrester Research, expects U.S. e-commerce sales alone to top $310 billion annually by 2010.

> *There are a number of pitfalls to be navigated in the commercial corners of cyberspace.*

Almost Anything Else

For obscure items in almost any category, eBay still leads the pack. While eBay has taken on almost mythic proportions in pop culture, its real presence is still pretty darn impressive. During just the first quarter of 2005, over 10 billion dollars worth of goods were traded there. With over 100 million registered users, industry analysts predict continued strong sales.

9.2 Shopping Problems

While 80% of online shoppers have been happy with their experiences, there are still a number of pitfalls to be navigated in the commercial corners of cyberspace. The most important, to most users, are understanding (and avoiding) data pharming, and protecting oneself from both online fraud and identity theft.

9.2.1 Data Pharmers

Data pharming is one of the dangers of shopping, or even browsing, online. We talked about data pharmers a bit in Chapter 8, "Taming the Cookie Monster." Simply put, a data pharmer is someone who farms the Internet, growing collections (databases) of information about Internet users.

This isn't always a bad thing. Some of the biggest names in online retailing collect a great deal of information about their buyers. These legitimate users never use the term *data pharming*. Instead, they simply "track preferences." Consider Amazon. If you're an Amazon buyer, chances are that Amazon knows a good bit about you and your online buying habits. They keep track of what you look at as well as what you buy. They track your purchases and even use that data to suggest other items that you'd probably be interested in. Netflix, the online movie rental company, does the same. When you rate movies on the Netflix site, they compile your ratings and use those to recommend similar movies that you'd probably like.

Often, this preference tracking can work to your advantage. I've found that over three-quarters of the movies that Netflix recommended to me were films that I'd already seen and liked or had planned to see eventually. Likewise, I've ordered at least a handful of Amazon's suggestions and been quite pleased with the results.

Where preference tracking becomes a problem is when you aren't aware that your preferences are being tracked, or you're not told who that data is being sold to or even that it is being sold. If you are aware that your online purchases are being tracked, remember to ask yourself, "How secure are the systems that keep track of what I buy?"

Most importantly, when you're considering a purchase with a new online site, find out what kind of privacy policies they have. Any legitimate site will have links from the home page (and most other pages), taking you directly to the privacy policy. Here's the Amazon Privacy Policy link, which appears at the bottom of every Amazon page:

`Conditions of Use | Privacy Notice © 1995-2005, Amazon.com, Inc. or its affiliates.`

That policy will tell you whether or not they sell information about you. Don't assume that if the privacy policy is front and center that your privacy is being protected. A very large number of e-commerce sites DO sell information about you and your purchases. They get away with that because most users never bother to read the posted privacy policy. Don't stay in the dark about where your information is going. Always read the privacy policy (see eBay's privacy policy in **Figure 9.1**). No privacy policy? Then there's probably no privacy either. I would strongly suggest you shop elsewhere.

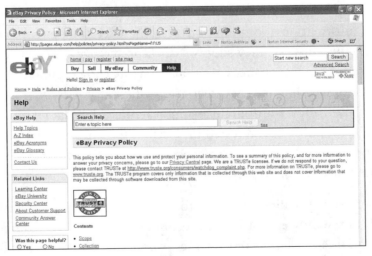

Figure 9.1
The eBay privacy policy

9.2.2 Hijackers

Unlike being pharmed, which can be good or bad, being hijacked is always a bad thing. What a hijacker does is send you to a different site than you think you're going to. You might believe you're at eToys.com when you're really looking at a well-spoofed site and handing your parent's credit card numbers to some con artist in Malaysia.

Hijacking   Rerouting users from the website they thought they were going to into a different (often spoofed) site without their knowledge.

Spoofing

Users can be tricked in several ways. You already know that fraudsters often spoof well-known sites that look like the real ones with a slightly different URL. Attackers send email and post links to these spoofed sites in the hopes that unsuspecting users will enter personal and financial information. We talked about this in Chapter 7, "Phishing for Dollars." This is becoming more common as phishing schemes proliferate, but it's thankfully easy to avoid. Simply NEVER go to a site by clicking on a link provided in an unsolicited email. Instead, type the URL as you know it in the address bar of your web browser (see **Figure 9.2**). Problem solved.

Figure 9.2

Note the URL typed directly into the address bar

Sometimes, however, the problem isn't a phishing scheme email so much as a user with poor spelling or typing skills. They type in the URL address themselves; they just don't spell it correctly. Spoofers select URLs that reflect common misspellings of commercial website URLs.

You can also avoid this problem by using the fraud-prevention tools now bundled into many security software packages. If your package doesn't include this protection, you can add it using a free program called SpoofStick. SpoofStick is a browser extension that you can download for Internet Explorer or the alternative browser Firefox. SpoofStick helps to detect spoofed websites.

For example, if you're on the following URL (and it's a legitimate Google URL), SpoofStick will say "You're on google.com," as shown in **Figure 9.3**. If you're on a fake website, SpoofStick will list the IP address rather than the company name you were expecting.

Figure 9.3
You really are on Google

You can download SpoofStick and install it in just a few minutes from a computer security company called CoreStreet at http://www.spoofstick.com/. Look to your security vendors to provide this software because it is critical that you know you are on the site you think you are on and that the site is trusted. That is, you can trust the site not to dump unwanted software onto your system. If you don't have anything right now, check with your vendor and, at minimum, download spoofstick. It does not tell if you if the site is trusted, but it will tell you if you landed on the correct site.

DNS Poisoning

The second way that users are hijacked is harder to avoid. It's called a **DNS poisoning**. DNS poisoning occurs when a hacker breaks into your local server. The server (spelled out Domain Name Server) is what translates the domain name you type into the correct numerical Internet address. You type in www.google.com, and it takes you to the specific Internet address where Google lives. This greatly simplifies using the Internet for you, since it's a lot easier to remember a mnemonic URL such as www.cnn.com than it is to remember an Internet address such as 192.123.0.0.

DNS Poisoning Compromising a domain name server to hijack users without even their web browsers catching on.

The problem with this system, and it is a serious problem, is that a compromised DNS server can wreak havoc on Internet users. If your DNS server is poisoned, you could actually type in the correct URL exactly the way it should be typed and still end up on some con artist's website. Even worse, your web browser would actually believe that you were on the legitimate site. There's no easy way to tell you've been hijacked.

While DNS poisoning is thankfully much less common than spoofing or computer viruses, it does happen. In October 2002, hackers succeeded in taking out 10 high-level DNS servers. Site-specific DNS poisoning attacks have taken aim at major online companies such as Google, eBay, and Amazon.

Even scarier, some relatively inexperienced hackers have taken up the habit as well. In September 2004, a German teenager managed to reroute traffic to the German eBay site, eBay.de. According to police spokesman Frank Federau, the boy wasn't even a computer expert. He told police he'd just stumbled across a website explaining the scam and thought he'd try it out "for fun." Given that he has since been charged with computer sabotage under German law, we can only hope he's reconsidered his idea of fun.

While it's harder to protect yourself from DNS poisoning than it is to avoid clicking on spoofed email links, it is still possible. You can minimize your chances of being victimized by limiting your e-commerce dealings to those sites having a valid digital certificate. I'll explain more about certificates in the next section, but for now just remember that the certificate should match the location you were trying to get to.

9.2.3 Online Fraud

Fraud is persistent and becoming more expensive. Online fraud includes purchased goods that fail to materialize, phony checks and electronic checks that never clear, work-at-home scams that never produce income for anyone but the scammer, and offers of "free" gifts and sweepstakes prizes that the user can claim only after paying shipping or taxes. In these cases, the prizes either never materialize or turn out to be worth substantially less than the handling fees required to collect them.

There's also a whole category of scams referred to as Nigerian money offers. A traditional Nigerian money offer is shown next. This is one of the longest running scams on the Internet, having started in the 1980s, and seems destined to continue almost in perpetuity. I have yet to meet anyone who's used the Net more than 6 or 8 months who hasn't received several of these offers. This scam is SO pervasive on the Net that the Financial Crimes Division of the Secret Service receives nearly 100 phone calls a day about it.

```
LAGOS, NIGERIA.
ATTENTION: THE PRESIDENT/CEO

DEAR SIR,

CONFIDENTIAL BUSINESS PROPOSAL

HAVING CONSULTED WITH MY COLLEAGUES AND BASED ON THE INFORMATION GATHERED FROM THE
NIGERIAN CHAMBERS OF COMMERCE AND INDUSTRY, I HAVE THE PRIVILEGE TO REQUEST FOR YOUR
ASSISTANCE TO TRANSFER THE SUM OF $47,500,000.00 (FORTY SEVEN MILLION, FIVE HUNDRED
THOUSAND UNITED STATES DOLLARS) INTO YOUR ACCOUNTS. THE ABOVE SUM RESULTED FROM AN OVER-
INVOICED CONTRACT, EXECUTED COMMISSIONED AND PAID FOR ABOUT FIVE YEARS (5) AGO BY A
FOREIGN CONTRACTOR. THIS ACTION WAS HOWEVER INTENTIONAL AND SINCE THEN THE FUND HAS BEEN
IN A SUSPENSE ACCOUNT AT THE CENTRAL BANK OF NIGERIA APEX BANK.

WE ARE NOW READY TO TRANSFER THE FUND OVERSEAS AND THAT IS WHERE YOU COME IN. IT IS
IMPORTANT TO INFORM YOU THAT AS CIVIL SERVANTS, WE ARE FORBIDDEN TO OPERATE A FOREIGN
ACCOUNT; THAT IS WHY WE REQUIRE YOUR ASSISTANCE. THE TOTAL SUM WILL BE SHARED AS
FOLLOWS: 70% FOR US, 25% FOR YOU AND 5% FOR LOCAL AND INTERNATIONAL EXPENSES INCIDENT TO
THE TRANSFER.
```

```
THE TRANSFER IS RISK FREE ON BOTH SIDES. I AM AN ACCOUNTANT WITH THE NIGERIAN NATIONAL
PETROLEUM CORPORATION (NNPC). IF YOU FIND THIS PROPOSAL ACCEPTABLE, WE SHALL REQUIRE THE
FOLLOWING DOCUMENTS:

(A) YOUR BANKER'S NAME, TELEPHONE, ACCOUNT AND FAX NUMBERS.

(B) YOUR PRIVATE TELEPHONE AND FAX NUMBERS -- FOR CONFIDENTIALITY AND EASY
COMMUNICATION.

(C) YOUR LETTER-HEADED PAPER STAMPED AND SIGNED.

ALTERNATIVELY WE WILL FURNISH YOU WITH THE TEXT OF WHAT TO TYPE INTO YOUR LETTER-HEADED
PAPER, ALONG WITH A BREAKDOWN EXPLAINING, COMPREHENSIVELY WHAT WE REQUIRE OF YOU. THE
BUSINESS WILL TAKE US THIRTY (30) WORKING DAYS TO ACCOMPLISH.

PLEASE REPLY URGENTLY.
BEST REGARDS
```

One of the best ways to keep your online purchasing experience pleasant is to limit your purchases to reputable sellers. Like many security measures, this is, of course, easier said than done. An easy first step, however, is to avoid buying anything from spammers. Nearly a quarter (24%) of Internet scams begin with unsolicited email.

Surprisingly, one in five online shoppers fails to follow this simple rule. A 2004 study by the Business Software Alliance (BSA) and the Council of Better Business Bureaus found that 21% of online shoppers had purchased software in response to spam email. Slightly more shoppers (22%) had bought clothing or jewelry in response to spam. While clothing quality is a bit harder to judge, software purchased in this way was often much less than satisfactory. It was also usually pirated.

While spam ads are pretty ubiquitous during most of the calendar year, the cyber-salesmen are out in force during the traditional pre-holiday shopping season. Before you bite on one of those too-good-to-be-true email offers, you might want to consider the advice of Bob Kruger, a vice president at BSA. He notes, "There are a lot of cyber-grinches out there who are only too happy to take consumers' money and spoil their holiday shopping season."

9.2.4 Identity Theft

In the long term, the biggest danger in purchasing from unscrupulous online sellers isn't that the goods will be shoddy. A larger danger is that the seller may even send you the goods but then sell your financial details or use them to steal your identity.

Identity theft is a nasty and growing practice. According to the Federal Trade Commission (FTC), 9.9 million Americans were victims of identity theft in 2002. While it's hard to put a price on the personal disaster of rebuilding your identity or credit history, these thefts cost financial institutions and businesses more than $48 million that year alone.

A lot of teens have the mistaken belief that they're really not at risk for identity theft. After all, it's not like you're a CEO of a major company or that you've got a stack of credit cards that some thief could get slap happy using. Big mistake. While teens may not carry 8 or 10 major credit cards, many carry—or have access to—at least one. Remember all those teen shoppers we just discussed?

Identity theft is a nasty and growing practice.

Well, they're not paying for online purchases with Yu-Gi-Oh! cards. While they may not have credit cards in their own names, many have their names on their parents' credit cards. (Not surprising given that Americans carry a total of over 640 million credit cards.) If your name is on even one credit card, you're at risk for identity theft. Even if it's not, the information you provide to online sellers could put your parents' identities at risk.

Mega-Losses!

In 2004, American victims of identity theft lost a total sum of $547 million.

Unscrupulous sellers and online scams are only one risk for identity theft. Some computer worms, such as MyTob, have remote-access capabilities that allow attackers to gather data stored on your PC. Other malicious code, such as the spyware, adware, and keyboard loggers we discussed in Chapter 2, "Drive-By Malicious Code," are also used to collect your private information and can eventually lead to identity theft. Remember, you need to have good anti-virus and anti-spyware software because the attackers are getting smart and are using platforms such as phishing attacks and the distribution of malicious code to steal confidential information using backdoors, bot networks, and keystroke loggers. Good anti-spyware software will detect keyboard loggers Above all, use common sense. Don't simply click on links. Many identity scams rely heavily on social engineering to trick you into giving up the goods. Remember that legitimate organizations never ask you to update your password or account information by sending email to you. And when they do contact you, they almost always address you by name.

As always, remember that your best defense is a good offense. Don't wait until you're older and settled financially to begin protecting your personal data. The time to start protecting your identity is the day you go online.

For your own protection, it is extremely important to keep track of your credit record. You can obtain a free copy of your credit report once a year by asking the credit bureau directly. The major credit reporting agencies are Experian, Equifax, and TransUnion. While they focus on different areas of the country, to be safe, request a credit report from each. And don't fall for companies advertising "free" credit reports if you sign up for their credit-checking services. Credit reports are always free once a year and you can check them at no charge ANYTIME you are denied credit or have reason to suspect fraud.

Undoing the Damage

If you or your parents become a victim of identity theft, it's important that you report the theft and begin cleaning up your history as soon as possible.

Before you do anything else, do the following:

- Contact the three major credit history reporting agencies (Experian, Equifax, and TransUnion) and place a fraud alert on your account. This will prevent the identity thief from opening any new accounts using your identity.

- Get a copy of your credit report. Contact all credit card issuers listed that you never actually opened an account with to have those accounts CLOSED.

- Call the Federal Trade Commission (FTC) at their identity theft hotline (1-800-IDTHEFT). They maintain a database of identity theft reports.

- Work with your parents to contact your local police department and file a report.

If you are too young to have a credit report, make sure you give these tips to your parents. They should be checking their credit reports REGULARLY to make sure their identity hasn't been compromised.

9.3 Ensuring Safe Shopping

While computer fraud has advanced in recent years, so has the technology that can help to protect the integrity of your online communications and financial transactions. Three of these technologies are especially important: encryption, authentication (SSL digital signatures, digital certificates), and security tokens.

9.3.1 Encryption

Encryption is a technique used to scramble content in files that you don't want anyone to be able to read. This protection is critical to safe online shopping. When you shop, you're sending a LOT of information that you really don't want to share with the general public—your credit card numbers and all your personal information, such as your full name, address, phone number(s), and email address(es). Encryption of one or more forms is crucial to protecting all that shopping information.

When you encrypt a file, you're applying a "code" to it so that anyone who doesn't know the code can't read the file. Unscrambling an encrypted file so that it's readable again is called *decrypting* it.

You can think of **encryption** as applying a type of secret code. Remember the codes you used to have to break for math class to learn logic? "Decode the secret message if A=1, B=2, C=3, etc." This is exactly like that.

Encryption Applying a secret code (cipher) to your messages or files to keep other people from reading them without your permission.

Let's use a simple code as an example. Let's say that we're going to encrypt a message by replacing every letter with the letter that precedes it in the alphabet. Every B becomes an A, every C becomes a B, etc. When you get back to the beginning, you wrap around so that every A becomes a Z. Using this code, let's encrypt the following phrase:

> This sentence is none of your business.

Once we apply our "cipher" (the alphabet precedence algorithm), this becomes:

> Sghr rdmsdmbd hr mnmd ne xntq atrhmdrr.

In computer terms, the first sentence, the one you can clearly understand, is called **plaintext**. This is your text, plain as day, just the way you entered it from your keyboard. The scrambled sentence at the bottom is called the **ciphertext**. That's your text once the encryption cipher (sometimes called the *cryptographic algorithm*) has been applied. If you don't know the cipher being applied, it's very difficult to figure out what the second sentence really means. So, it's extremely hard to decrypt the ciphertext. Trying to break an encrypted message without authorization is called cryptoanalysis.

Plaintext   The plain, clearly readable text message before encryption.

Of course, computer ciphers are an awful lot more complicated than our sample code. Most use at least a 64-bit encryption (often 128-bit). That means that the cipher key (that's a type of password that determines the cryptographic algorithm applied to encrypt your text) has at least 64 digits—possible many more—that need to be puzzled out in the correct sequence for a code breaker to have any hope of decrypting your message without your permission.

In Internet security terms though, even 64-bit encryption is considered pretty simple—in fact, almost lame. Larger keys are used to produce stronger encryption. In general terms, encryption strength is measured by the encryption algorithm and the size of the key. A bigger key usually means stronger encryption.

Cryptoanalysis   Trying to break an encrypted message without authorization.

In addition to encryption key size, encryption methods also vary. Today, there are two major methods used to encrypt communications over the Internet: symmetric encryption and public key encryption. Symmetric encryption, also called *secret key encryption*, uses the same key to encrypt and decrypt the message. In symmetric encryption, both the sender and the receiver have to have the same key. Therefore, the key must be kept secret. Public key encryption uses two keys: a public key and a private key. You can use either key to encrypt the message, but only one of the keys will decrypt the message.

Ciphertext A message or file after it has been encrypted. Ciphertext appears garbled and can't be read until it's decrypted.

What all of these methods have in common, though, is that you MUST have the cipher or key to translate the ciphertext back into plaintext that makes sense. No key, no content.

As you might imagine, cryptography and the art of computer encryption are pretty complicated as well as just being pretty cool. If you'd like to learn more about this topic, I suggest you read *Applied Cryptography* by Bruce Schneier.

Common Codes and Dead Cows

Ciphers—secret codes—are pretty common on the Net. IM speak ("R u hm" for "Are you home?") is one example of a common online cipher.

Another popular code is called 1337 (and pronounced "leet"), named for the 1337 (numerical) port used for an infamous computer attack by the hacker group that calls itself the Cult of the Dead Cow.

In 1337, words are spelled using numbers and symbols to replace the letters that they physically resemble. A simple example would be:

`1337 h4x0rz un j00!` → `Elite hackers own you!`

Fluent 1337 sp33k3rz get even more obscure, replacing R's with "/2", etc. and making some pretty wild substitutes for other letters such as M, N, and W:

`_|00 |2 4/\/ (_)83|2 |-|4><0|2!` → `You are an uber hacker!`

Also note that while many 1337 comments are insults (something about the gaming culture?), you can also use 1337 to send hugs and kisses, `><><><()()><><><()()()`, and love, `<3` !

9.3.2 Secure Socket Layer (SSL)

SSL is an important layer of security if you are providing personal information such as during a transaction. SSL is a protocol that encrypts the transmission of data via HTTP. You can tell if you are protected by SSL if the browser bar has an *https* instead of *http*, and if you see the lock on the bottom right of your web browser.

9.3.3 Digital Signatures, Certificates, and Hashing

While encryption protects the contents of your message, it does nothing to prove or verify that you're the person who actually sent it. This process of proving the source of a message or website is called **authentication**.

When you're shopping online, authentication is a pretty important concept. Before you hand over your parents' credit cards numbers to L.L. Bean to order that really cool winter ski jacket, you want to make sure that it really is L.L. Bean that you're talking to. In that case, while you still want and need to have those credit card numbers encrypted, you also want and need to authenticate the recipient.

> **Who Provides What?**
>
> While I talk about using digital signatures, etc., to improve security, you really don't need to USE these items per se. Legitimate retailers know you're concerned about potential fraud. So, THEY provide things like digital signatures and certificates to prove to you that they're who they say they are.

Authentication   Verifying the identity of a message sender or website.

Three common methods are used for authentication: hashing, digital signatures, and digital certificates.

Hashing

Hashing, most commonly a one-way hash, is a method used to verify data rather than encrypt it. With this method, a one-way hash algorithm is applied to the plaintext. The result is a "message digest" attached to the original plaintext message. This digest functions as a unique, identifiable "fingerprint" for the message. If the message is changed in any way, applying the one-way algorithm will generate a "fingerprint" that no longer matches the attached digest. This process allows the message recipient to check the plaintext message received against the message digest to ensure the file was not tampered with.

Digital Signatures

A digital signature is another method used to verify the sender of a message. Unlike hashing, digital signatures do use encryption (specifically, a type of public key encryption, which uses two algorithms—one for encrypting and the other for decrypting the digital signature).

In simple terms then, a digital signature is attached to encrypted data to ensure two things: (1) that the message is authentic and intact, and (2) to authenticate the message sender. Thus, using a digital signature has the same effect as using hashing along with encryption. It simply does so using a slightly different methodology.

Digital Certificates

A digital certificate takes the digital signature concept to a higher and much more secure level, by adding a trusted third party. When you buy something over the Internet—for example, from Amazon.com—you are using public key infrastructure. The problem with using only public key encryption in this case is that anyone can create a public/private key pair. It's a bit complicated, but the basic idea is that it is possible to "forge" a digital signature. The signature itself would still match (the public/private key combination would still work), but the signature author might not be who you thought it was.

> You can think of a digital certificate as being analogous to a driver's license.

To avoid the problem of forged digital signatures, most major e-commerce retailers instead make use of a digital certificate. A digital certificate contains a person's or corporation's public key. This is exactly like a digital signature. The difference is that a digital certificate is issued by a trusted third party who verifies independently that the certificate belongs to the person claiming ownership.

You can think of a digital certificate as being analogous to a driver's license. When you obtain a driver's license, you have to provide reasonable identification to the Department of Motor Vehicles (DMV). The companies that issue digital certificates, such as VeriSign, function as the DMV and obtain that reasonable identification. VeriSign's certification authority (CA) then issues a public/private key pair (for a small fee), keeps the matching public key in a database, issues a digital certificate, and keeps a copy of the certificate in its database.

Sometimes you will be given the option of accepting or rejecting a digital certificate.

9.3.4 Security Tokens

Encryption protects the contents of your messages and files. Hashing, digital signatures, and digital certificates authenticate the people and places that you're doing business with. **Security tokens**, on the other hand, actually authenticate YOU.

You're probably thinking, "But I do that myself when I enter my private password." True. The problem is that passwords can be easily cracked and stolen by hackers. Security tokens provide a much stronger method of authentication by using two-factor authentication that includes both data (often a password) and a physical device.

Two-factor authentication is something that you probably already use all the time offline. When you use an ATM card to withdraw money from your bank account, you're using two-factor authentication. The physical ATM card itself identifies you (factor one), as does the PIN number that you enter (factor two). While it's important that you don't misplace either, neither is really useful without the other. A criminal can play with your ATM card all day, but he's not getting money from your bank unless he also knows your PIN number.

Security Token   A two-factor authentication method using a physical device as well as a secret code.

An ATM card is only one example of a security token. Other forms of security tokens are physical tokens (a small hardware device), smart cards, and biometric systems. With biometrics, the physical component is the biological data (such as a fingerprint scan) that you provide.

While security tokens are currently used less often than digital signatures or certificates, most experts see them as most definitely the wave of the future.

Chapter 10

Private Blogs and Public Places

Not-So-Secret Diaries

I spent this morning reading my oldest daughter's online diary. And that of her younger sister. Her cousins. Her best friends. Her boyfriend...

How'd I get there? I did a 5-second Yahoo! search on my daughter's boyfriend's name. The first site that came up was his Xanga blog. It didn't take long clicking through his Subscriptions to find my daughter's blog. From her blog, I meandered through the online musings of her friends. And their friends. Each new blog gave me links to the next. I'm starting to feel like I've spent the morning reading the diaries of half the kids in this county.

IN THE SUMMER, I VOLUNTEER WITH HABITAT FOR HUMANITY.

THAT'S FUNNY. YOUR MYSPACE PAGE SAYS YOU SLEEP IN UNTIL NOON...

I won't tell them, of course. None of them gave me their links and I'm ABSOLUTELY sure they weren't meaning for me to read the stuff they posted. The content was really eye-opening. I'm still floored by some of the incredibly personal things the kids said. It's like they think they're the only people living on the Net. I wonder how teens will feel about those same comments when they've grown up but their online comments live forever in cyberspace...

—*Anonymous mom*

Unless you're a pretty atypical teen, chances are that you already have an online blog or know someone who does. Twenty percent of American teens already keep a blog, and that number increases each day. You may have opened your blog in response to reading a friend's and never really considered the implications of having one. Have you thought about what types of things it's OK to post? Or wondered what will happen to your blog entries in years to come?

In this chapter, I'll talk about the implications of having an online blog and how to do so without compromising your safety or your future. I'll also talk about the history of the blogging community.

10.1 So What's a Blog?

Blog is short for "weblog"—a website that consists of a series of data entries. Much like an online journal or diary, some blogs are standalone. That is, they don't link to other sites. However, most blogs contain links to other blogs and sites of interest. While it can look, and sometimes function, as a private diary, a blog is really a very public record. In fact, one of the problems with blogs in terms of protecting individual privacy is that too many users seem to treat them as if they really were private diaries instead of public records.

Blog   A web-based log containing text entries ordered by date (like a journal) as well as links to other sites.

In industry terms, blogs are a fairly recent phenomenon, dating only from the mid- to late-1990s. According to some experts, the first blog appeared in 1993, but there's some question whether Mosaic's What's New Page really meets the criteria of a blog as we understand it today. While it certainly did contain the expected links to other sites of interest, it also lacked the personal "diary-style" touch that defines the essence of today's blogs.

Personally, I'd date the first blog to 1997. That was when John Barger actually coined to term *weblog* to describe his Robot Wisdom Weblog. Another blogger, Peter Merholz, later shortened "weblog" to create the term *blog* that we use today. As you'll note from the incredibly hard-to-read screenshot shown in **Figure 10.1**, this was long before the advent of the free weblog-creation programs that simplify creating crisp web pages that are easy to read and navigate.

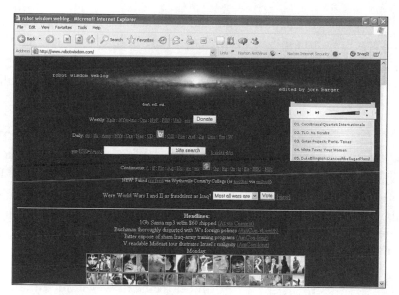

Figure 10.1
John Barger's Robot Wisdom Weblog (http://www.robotwisdom.com/)

Today, blogs are much more polished and considerably easier to create. With the advent of free blog-creation programs, bloggers no longer need to understand the Hypertext Markup Language (HTML) used to create web pages—or really have any knowledge of even basic web page creation.

HTML (Hypertext Markup Language)   The language used to create web pages.

As the process has become simpler, the number of blogs being created has increased exponentially. For teenagers, blogging has become almost a rite of passage. A 2003 study by Perseus Development Corporation found that over half of blogs are authored by teenagers.

10.2 Blogging Makes the Big Time

While blogging dates to the mid-1990s, it didn't really take off until Pyra released the tool Blogger, which allowed less-savvy users to create and maintain blogs without becoming webmasters in the process. Blogger expanded the blogging community from a few dozen techno-elites and opened the door for the rest of the Internet community.

The rush of would-be-bloggers through that door was astounding. According to Technorati, a tracking firm in San Francisco, a new blog or two is created just about every second of every day. That's 100,000 new blogs a day, joining the 20 million+ blogs already out there. One in five American teens keeps an online blog, and even more, 38%, read others' blogs.

Top Teen Blogs

If you're looking to create your own blog, or just want to read blogs probably written by other teens, here are a few good recommendations on where to go:

- MySpace
- Xanga
- LifeJournal
- Friendster

Using this forum, bloggers discuss everything from yesterday's social studies test to international events and national policy. Political blogs have taken off to the point that in 2004 a number of bloggers were issued official press passes to cover the major party conventions preceding the presidential elections.

For most teens, however, maintaining a blog rates much closer to keeping a public journal than being part of the media establishment. As such, teens tend to keep their blogs within mostly teen-friendly environments.

10.3 Say WHAT?!!!

Blogging has become an apparently permanent part of the teen culture. That's not necessarily a bad thing. Teens have some pretty intense philosophical discussions in some of those blogs. Kevin Krim, head of subscriptions at the company that owns blog site *LifeJournal*, points out, "For every off-color picture you might find, you are also going to find a number of kids having really interesting conversations about their developing views of spirituality, what they think about war. Those are good things to be thinking about."

The trick with blogs, as with all areas of Internet technology, is to keep the good while avoiding the clearly bad or dangerous. The good part is that blogs provide an easy, motivating forum in which teens hone their wit, unknowingly practice their writing skills, and essentially document their adolescence. However, as Elizabeth Armstrong pointed out in the *Christian Science Monitor*, while a blog may be an easy online diary, it's a diary to which "the rest of the world now has peeping rights."

With blogging and in digital neighborhoods (such as MySpace), a truly dangerous area is that kids provide FAR too much personal information. A study published in 2005 by the Children's Digital Media Center at Georgetown University reported that 20% of underage bloggers include their full names on their sites. Over half (60%) publish their locations and contact information. If the only people reading their blogs were other teens, that might be OK. Of course, they aren't. Remember the bad guys we discussed in Chapter 6, "Pretenders and Pirates?"

> ### Blogging No-No's
>
> Be a safety-conscious blogger! Never post:
>
> - Your full name
> - Your address
> - Your phone number
> - Your age
> - Anything you wouldn't want your mother to see!
>
> Also, don't smear other teens or attack their reputations with your posts.

Putting personally identifying information in your blog is no different than discussing personal details in a chat room. This can put you at considerable risk from unsavory characters online. Don't think they're there? Ask Cara Cabral, a 17-year-old high school student. She complains of older men trying to meet teenage girls. According to Cara, "They're just real creepy. You'll find that the strangest people will want to be your friend on MySpace.com."

Of course, there's always the danger of creepy characters anyplace a large number of teens gather. And blogs are certainly one of those places. Mary Ellen Handy, a middle school technology coordinator, reports that a full third of her 250 students keep blogs. That's expected. What's frightening is that only 5% of those students' parents knew that. While that low number might surprise you, it undoubtedly wouldn't surprise Edward Parmelee, a special agent with the FBI's Jackson, Mississippi cyber-crime squad. A frequent speaker at schools, Parmelee notes that when he mentions blogging to parent groups, "We get these deer-in-headlights stares. They don't even know what we're talking about."

If your parents are among the uninformed, this could be your chance to bring them up to speed. While you may not want them reading your own blog on a regular basis, keep in mind that your parents are your first and best defense. You should keep them in the loop enough to allow them to help you make good decisions for your own protection.

10.4 Object Permanence

Another problem with the proliferation of teen blogs is that most teens have no idea just how long those blogs will be around. That could be a very, very long time.

If you're wondering just how long those old blog entries you've made can hang around, have a look at **Figure 10.2**. These are the entries made on Mosaic's What's New page at its inception back in 1993. Chances are that you were still in diapers when these entries were first blogged!

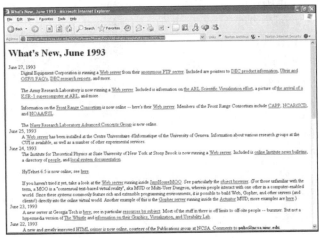

Figure 10.2

Mosaic's What's New page, June 1993 (http://archive.ncsa.uiuc.edu/SDG/Software/ Mosaic/Docs/old-whats-new/whats-new-0693.html)

Unlike physical diaries or journals, blog entries are public creatures, not private. Once you've added a new entry to your blog, those words become easily accessible to nearly every person on earth who has Internet access. Many blogs are completely open, not even requiring readers to log in. Xanga.com, a popular teen blogging site, is exactly like that. The anonymous mom in our case study at the front of the chapter didn't need to actually log into Xanga to read her teen's online postings. She simply ran a quick Yahoo! search.

Even sticking to sites that limit access to other members hardly restricts access to your blog entries. Just how difficult was it for you to open a blogger's account at MySpace? What makes you think that your mom, your school principal, or even a prospective employer 10 years from now couldn't do the same?

10.5 Bloggers Eat Their Own

While teens maintain blogs that are often a bit too personal, they are still—for the most part—fairly positive. Some of the supposed grown-ups in the **blogosphere** aren't quite so well behaved. An unfortunate side effect of the growth of the blogging culture has been the emergence of the attack blog.

Blogosphere   The blogging community as a whole. This includes all sets of blogging forums, blogging sites, and individually maintained blogs.

Attack blogs exist partly, and sometimes wholly, to say unpleasant things about others. Sometimes they attack political adversaries. Other times, they take aim at competitors. Or simply people or products the blog writer just doesn't like. Attacking others through online blogs can be seriously damaging. Olivia, a teen in Novato, California, was attacked by a group of other teens in an online blog on MySpacc.com. The blogs were so cruel and damaging that her mom had to transfer her to another school. That's just not right. Attack blogs are not a problem for teens only.

The attack nature of some political blogs is hardly surprising. Politicians and political commentators have never really been known for their restraint when it comes to slinging mud at their opponents. Al Franken, a well-known political commentator and humorist from the left, set a good example of that tone in his 1999 book *Rush Limbaugh Is a Big Fat Idiot*. (Limbaugh is a well-known political commentator from the right.) While Franken was considerably less than kind in his accusations, he did at least back them up with factual evidence. Many bloggers make considerably nastier accusations with little or no facts to back them up.

Where attack blogs have come into their own, isn't so much in making political statements but in attacking unpopular corporations. Popular targets such as Microsoft and IBM find themselves fending off some very mean and untrue accusations. Luckily, corporate strength gives them added resiliency.

10.5.1 Negative Logs, Blogs, and Websites

It's not only corporations that deal with the effects of negative attacks. In a head-lined article about MySpace on March 27, 2006 in the Marin IJ, "It's fun and real simple, and for somebody you met at camp, it's great to keep in touch with really well," said 14-year-old Tessa of San Rafael. "People don't write letters anymore."

MySpace has been a nightmare for one student reported in the Marin IJ. A teen at Hill Middle School, in Novato, California, had to transfer to another school because of other classmates who put up a hate website on MySpace that specifi-cally targeted this teen in a bad way. I hope MySpace bans teens forever from the site when they post hate material about another teen. Don't bully other kids online. Think of how you would feel if someone started putting hate material on the Inter-net about you. It's just not right. Don't do it.

10.5.2 Legal Repercussions

Another good reason not to respond to nasty blogs is that you don't want to be dragged into any ensuing legal battles. When adults begin throwing unsupported accusations at each other, the inclination on all sides is to run for a lawyer.

Libel (publishing statements that you know to be untrue) is not only ungracious, it's illegal. If you're convicted of libel, you could find yourself liable to pay for any damage that you caused to your victim's reputation or livelihood. This can be very, very expensive. Let's imagine that you decide to really trash a company's new weight-loss product. You announce in your blog that not only did you not lose any weight, but you blew up like a balloon and developed a nasty rash across your face. You even post a photo of poor you with the horrible rash that was all their fault. Now, let's imagine that you actually got that swelling and rash by being stung by a wasp. You just used the picture to get back at them because you read somewhere that they were still using animal testing on their products. Your mo-tives might have been honorable, but your postings still constituted libel. If they sued you (and they just might if you damaged their sales enough), you could be on the hook for all the money they MIGHT have made in the next 20 years if the reputation of their product hadn't been trashed.

Are you likely to be convicted for nasty comments that you make in your blog? Probably not. On the other hand, you're not likely to go to jail for stealing your neighbor's newspaper every morning. Keeping your web postings honest (and your hands off of your neighbor's news) is just the right thing to do.

10.5.3 Getting What You Give

An even more important reason to stay out of nasty blogs is that some bloggers are an awful lot like those swarms of feeding frenzied sharks. Drop enough blood in the water and they may turn around and attack their own.

If you want to hush up a nasty rumor, it's probably not in your best interests to scream back at someone sitting on a very large and very public soap box. And, that's a pretty good description of where attack bloggers sit.

This is something to think about if you find yourself considering, or you are in the midst of, a blog battle. Take the advice of Robert Mahaffey, a cyber-crime investigator for the Mississippi Attorney General's office. "The Internet is the wild, wild West of the 21st century, and it should be viewed that way." Thankfully, attack bloggers are a very small minority of the blogging community. Mahaffey points that out himself, noting that "Attack blogs are but a sliver of the rapidly expanding blogosphere." Of course, gunslingers and outlaws were also a small part of the old West. That didn't mean that they weren't a real threat. Attack bloggers are a similarly dangerous minority. Taunting them by posting back definitely isn't very wise.

10.6 Thinking Ahead

Like email (which often stays on your ISP's mail servers long after you've deleted your copy and forgotten
its content), blog entries also don't really go away when
you've moved on and forgotten about them. They live on
in backup drives and archive files. They may even live on
sitting on someone else's website. How often have you
copied something you found especially profound or funny
and pasted it into your own website? Someone else out there (or many someones)
may have done the same thing with your postings.

> *Blog entries don't really go away when you've moved on and forgotten about them.*

Throughout history, teens have done and said stupid things they've come to regret
as they entered into adulthood. I know I did. What's changed is that blogs, movie
clips, and IM logs document those mistakes—maybe forever. That's a long time.

Think about some of the silly or downright stupid things that you've done in the
past year. Now you can even put those downright stupid things into mini movie
clips and share them with your friends and the world. The teen movie clip site
www.youtube.com is a place where teens do just that. IM clients also have video
capability, and it's not necessarily private—it can be intercepted. You might be
sending something you think is private and it gets out to the world. These mini
movie clips can stay around for years just like blogs and can be just as damaging
to your reputation 5, 10, 30 years after the making. Do you want the world to see
your mini movie when you're 30? What about when you are looking for a job?
Did you know that some employers do research on the candidate on MySpace and
throughout the Internet before making the decision to hire the candidate?

In recent history, a number of persons nominated to the U.S. Supreme Court have
been forced to withdraw over allegations of poor decisions that they made in the
1960s. Just imagine if those decisions had been documented online in blogs or
movie clips by the nominees themselves. In 30 years we could have Congressio-
nal Committees skip the FBI checks on prospective judges and turn instead to the
archives files of old blogs and movie clips. Given some of the teen blogs I've read
lately, I can envision a Supreme Court filled with nine empty chairs. At the very
least, there'd be an awful lot of thoroughly embarrassed grandparents. Don't be
one of them.

10.7 The Right Way to Post Information

Reading back over this chapter, it's struck me that I probably seem a bit negative. A little too much of the "big hairy monsters on the Internet" tone. Because my job in this book is to protect you from the nasty side of cyberspace, that's a little unavoidable.

Still, I don't want to leave you with the idea that blogging is a bad thing. It's not. My own kids blog early and often. Their blogs, like their IM buddy lists, are an important part of their online existence. Their entries over time show a clear record of their magical growth, a web-based documentary of their development into thoughtful, exciting, educated adults.

Your own blog could easily do the same. To take advantage of the boons of the digital neighborhoods, you just need to follow a few simple rules:

- **Be honest.** This means you should maintain your integrity on several levels. Obviously, you should only publish blog entries and information you know to be true. You should also be honest about yourself. If you need to lie about your age to participate in a particular blogging forum, you know in your heart that you really shouldn't be there. There are blogs that are open to teens of all ages. For your own protection, stay out of the forums intended only for adults and teens older than you.

- **Don't be too honest.** There are some things your blog audience really doesn't need to know. These include any bits of information that would personally identify you. Your name. Your address or even the name of your town. Your school name. The full names of any friends or acquaintances. For your own protection, you need to keep your personal information OFF the Net.

- **Use discretion.** Always remember that your blog and web page are PUBLIC records. Don't post anything you wouldn't be comfortable sharing with Grandma over dinner at Thanksgiving.

- **Think ahead.** Never forget that your blog entries may very well outlive you. Before you post something, ask yourself how you'll feel about that entry next month or next year. Or well into the next decade.

- **If you can't say anything nice, don't say it at all.** Stay away from attack blogs and watch how you treat others online.

Chapter 11

Any Port in a Storm

Don't F.E.A.R. the Firewall

It was Friday evening, prime time for playing rounds of online games and chatting away on Instant Messenger with friends from school. Douglas, a 15-year-old boy from Novato, California, had—as usual—gone straight from the dinner table to the Net.

Douglas is a serious gamer. He has every game system on the market. He even has two 360s in his bedroom. Needless to say he also spends time playing his favorite game, F.E.A.R., on the Internet. In the middle of the game he lost his connection and was dropped from the gaming site. Douglas said, "That's not right. What the heck?" The following message flashed across his computer screen.

```
Connection Lost Out of Bandwidth!!!
```

Douglas thought that it was bad enough to not be able to finish the game but he had no clue what that message meant. Douglas started to wonder if he'd been dropped off because of the firewall on his parent's network. Douglas turned off the firewall, entered the gaming site and began to play his favorite game again. No drop off this time. Douglas simply decided to leave the firewall off while he was playing his game on the Internet.

While turning off the firewall sounded like a good idea to Douglas, that was not the problem. It created a new problem because turning off the firewall opened the door to his parents' home network to hackers. The bandwidth problem had to do with the network in Douglas's house. He simply did not have enough bandwidth coming into his house in the first place. In this chapter, you will see how you can test your bandwidth for free. Also, this chapter talks about some of the basics of networking and why firewalls are a critical component of security that you simply cannot live without.

11.1 So What's a Network?

A computer network is a group of computers that are connected. Sometimes this is a physical connection using wires, cables, telephone lines, or some combination of the three. Sometimes there is no physical connection. (Think about "hot spots" and wireless networks here.) The point is that the computers within a network are connected in a way that allows their users to share resources such as files and/or physical devices such as printers.

> *In this chapter, you will see how you can test your bandwidth for free.*

Computer networks come in many shapes and sizes. They can be HUGE. A major university might have a computer network that connects tens of thousands of students, faculty, and staff. A computer network can also be quite small. The network I've installed in my house connects six computers. Because we're using network technology, all of us can use the same Internet connection and send files to the same printer.

Protocol   A set of rules that computers use to communicate with each other.

Regardless of their size, all networks work pretty much the same way and provide the same functions. That is, they all use one **protocol** or another to allow the computers and other devices in the network to talk to each other, and they all provide shared access to network resources (see **Figure 11.1**).

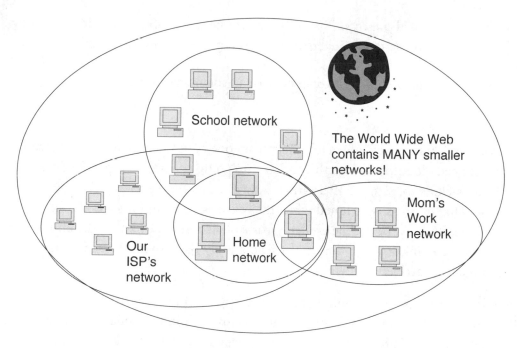

Figure 11.1
The world is literally filled with computer networks!

11.2 How Networks Communicate—TCP/IP

Being part of a network is like being part of a community. In a community, life runs smoothly only when the people who form the community talk to each other. In order to share community resources, the members of the community need to communicate in ways that everyone can understand.

Computer networks are much the same. In order for the computers to share resources, they need to communicate using a common language. In computer terms, that common language is called a **protocol**. A protocol is a set of rules that computers use to communicate with each other.

TCP/IP is the protocol that is used most often to communicate on the Internet. TCP stands for *Transmission Control Protocol*. TCP is the protocol that controls how things are transmitted on the Internet. In specifics, TCP works by sending data in blocks called *packets*. IP stands for *Internet Protocol*, and it describes how computers send those data packets from one computer to another.

TCP/IP The protocol that most computers use to communicate on the Internet.

11.2.1 IP Addresses

In order for data packets to travel safely from one computer to another, the control protocol needs to know where the packets are going to—it needs an IP address to send the packets to. A static IP address is always exactly the same, like your house address. That address is assigned when the house is built and it stays the same as long as the house is there. The control protocol also needs to know the address the packets are coming from so that it can send a reply back to let the sender know that everything arrived safely.

Just like your house has a mailing address, every computer on the Internet has an IP address. Each IP address contains four groups of numbers separated by periods. For example, 192.168.1.1 is an IP address. Depending on what kind of Internet connection you have and how your ISP assigns addresses, you may have a static IP address or a dynamic IP address.

While your house address is assigned by the post office, your computer's IP address is assigned by your Internet Service Provider (ISP), or possibly by indirectly connected machines if you have a private home network.

ISP (Internet Service Provider) This is the company that provides the network that allows your computer to connect to the Internet.

The advantage of having a static address for your house is that once a person learns your address, that person will always know your address. With IP addresses, this is a disadvantage as well as an advantage. The disadvantage is that once a hacker learns a static IP address, he would always know how to get back to that specific computer. However, ISPs also issue dynamic IP addresses.

A dynamic IP address is issued when you connect to the Internet on any given day and you keep that address only until you shut down your computer and router.

The next time you connect to the Internet, you get a new (and probably different) IP address. Dynamic IP addresses may help protect you from being targeted repeatedly by a hacker trying to break into your computer. When it comes to dynamic addresses, your ISP assigns addresses from a pool of addresses that it uses. The protocol that manages the assignment of IP addresses is called **DHCP (Dynamic Host Configuration Protocol)**.

DHCP (Dynamic Host Configuration Protocol)   The protocol that an ISP uses to assign dynamic IP addresses.

Whether you have a static IP address or a dynamic IP address depends on two things: (1) what type of Internet connection you have, and (2) the policies of your ISP. If you have a dial-up connection (using the phone line), you definitely have a dynamic IP address.

If your connection is always on, and you have a static IP address, attackers have a better chance of being successful at attacking you. It's simple to see that if you always have the same IP address you are easier to find. That does not mean that dynamic IP addresses are safe, however. You still need a firewall. We'll talk about firewalls in detail later in this chapter. For now, just know that a firewall helps to keep the bad guys from walking in your front door as well as using back doors to access your computer system.

To find your IP address, first make sure that your computer is connected to the Internet. Then click **Start**, click **Run**, type **cmd**, and click **OK**. This will give you a DOS window, sometimes called a *command prompt* or *C: prompt*.

Enter the **ipconfig /all** command at end of the C:\...> (DOS) prompt line. The window that displays next will list your IP address.

You can simply type in the IPCONFIG command if you only want to see your IP address. I wanted to show you that I have a dynamic IP address. If you have a DHCP address, the IPCONFIG /ALL command shows you the lease time. I have a 24-hour lease time, a dynamic IP address. Next time I shut down my computer and router, I likely will be issued a different IP address.

You can also find the IP addresses for other computer systems by using the nslookup command. For example, to find the IP address for Google, click on **Start, Run, cmd, OK** to again open a command prompt window. Then, enter the command **nslookup www.google.com**.

As I've said, an IP address is similar to your home address. Once you have an address to a house, you can knock on the door and you might get in. When you find the IP address to a computer system, you've basically found the front door. Several layers of defense are needed to protect your network. For example, to protect your front door, you need to use a firewall.

Also, a simple step you can take to protect your computer when you are not using it is to simply turn off your computer and router when you're not using them. Think about it. Hackers know that many home users just keep the systems always on and connected to the Internet because it's so convenient. Therefore, it makes sense to turn off your computer and router when you are not connected to the Internet.

> *A simple step that you can take to protect your computer is to simply turn off your computer and router when you're not using them.*

11.2.2 Data Packets

TCP/IP works by splitting messages and files being sent over the Internet into chunks that are called *packets*. Each packet contains part of the message or file, plus the address of its destination.

In this type of communication, the computers sending data back and forth are called *hosts*. The computer sending the packet is called the *source host*. The computer receiving the packet is called the *destination host*. Both hosts use the protocol to make sure that the packets arrive safely and in the right order.

Imagine that you were sending a book that you'd written on computer gaming from your computer to your teacher's computer. When you send the file containing the book, the controlling protocol would first split the book into smaller sections (packets). While actual data packets are considerably smaller, to make this simple let's imagine that each chapter becomes a packet. If there are six chapters in your book, there might be six data packets. Each packet would contain a separate chapter plus the IP address of your teacher's computer.

The control protocol would also add sequence information (say, the page number) to make sure that when the packets are assembled back into a single file at your teacher's computer, the chapters are still in the correct order. This makes sure that Chapter 1 comes first, Chapter 2 second, etc. To make things even more reliable, the control protocol on your teacher's computer would send a confirmation back to your computer, letting it know that the packets arrived safely.

11.2.3 Confirmation

There are actually a number of protocols that computers could use to communicate. TCP/IP is simply the most common. Some communications use a different protocol called UDP instead. Most Internet connections, however, use TCP/IP because it's considered to be more reliable.

TCP is considered to be a reliable connection because the computer sending the data receives confirmation that the data was actually sent. UDP doesn't send confirmations. This makes UDP faster than TCP but not quite as reliable. In some cases, that's OK. Knowing that something actually made it to the destination is important for some programs, and not for others.

11.3 Port of Call

Whereas an IP address identifies the location of your computer, the locations through which data actually gets into your computer are called *ports*. You can think of a port as a door into your computer.

Unlike your house, which probably has only two or three external doors, your computer has many, many doors. Computers have a total of 65,535 ports. Some of these ports are allocated to specific applications. For example, AOL Instant Messenger uses port 5190. HTTP, the protocol used to communicate web pages, runs on port 80 and port 8080.

When I say that an application runs on a specific port, what I really mean is that the application uses a service program to monitor that port. Thus, IM runs a service that hangs out at port 5190. It listens at that port for communications to arrive and responds when it detects those communications. You can think of these services as doormen. They wait at the door to see who knocks. When someone does knock (that is, data arrives at that port), the doormen (services) follow the rules (protocol) they've been given to decide whether or not to let the knockers in.

11.3.1 Port Scanning

Attackers routinely scan the Internet looking for computers with open (unprotected) ports. This is called **port scanning**.

Port Scanning   Searching the Internet for computers with open ports.

As you learned earlier, some applications run on specific ports. Of course, there are 65,535 available ports. You can specify access for services on specific ports through your firewall. Your firewall functions as a bouncer at an exclusive club; your firewall has a "guest list" of exactly who is allowed in at which port. Thus, firewalls block access to ports that are not being used for specific applications. A firewall that is configured correctly won't accept connections to ports unless it's specifically told to do so. To protect your computer and its data, you need to make sure that your ports are protected. The list of ports and services are too extensive to cover here. You should visit your firewall vendor's site to see what ports and services are recommended and which ones are considered risky. Another good place to learn about ports and services is GRC.com.

11.4 A Bit More about Bandwidth

Bandwidth is the speed at which data is sent over a communication line. Bandwidth measures how quickly your PC communicates with the Internet. Douglas was dropped from the game he was playing over the Internet when the message "You are out of bandwidth" flashed across the screen. Unfortunately, Douglas simply did not have enough bandwidth coming into his house. Do you know how much bandwidth you have?

Douglas's mom was paying her cable provider for 3 megabits per second. When they were not getting enough bandwidth into the house, Douglas's mom checked to see just how much bandwidth she was getting. It turned out only 1.7 megabits was available. She was paying for more than what she was getting. Douglas's mom called her cable provider and yelled at them for not providing what they were supposed to. They immediately coughed up the extra bandwidth. You need to know what you are paying for and make sure that's what's coming into your house. It's simple and free to test.

There are a number of places on the Internet where you can run a bandwidth test on your system for free. One such safe site is www.bandwidthplace.com.

Your potential bandwidth will depend on the type of Internet connection that you have.

11.5 Rings of Fire

Using a firewall does NOT eliminate your need for other security products.

When you started this book, you probably had no idea you had 65,535 available ports on your computer. Watching and blocking those doors to your computer is one of the most important security jobs you need to fill. We've already talked about a number of products and techniques you can use to protect your computer. A firewall is *one more* important layer of defense.

While you absolutely NEED a firewall, keep in mind that it is only *one* piece of the security protection puzzle. Using a firewall does NOT eliminate your need for other security products such as antivirus and anti-spyware programs, unless your firewall comes as part of a bundled security solution. (Some security products aim to provide a total or near-total "solution" to security problems by bundling a whole bunch of different types of protective software into a single product. For more information about bundled solutions, please read Chapter 13, "Protective Tools.")

This part of the chapter talks about why firewalls are essential and provides details on what firewalls can and can't do. By the end of this chapter, you should have learned enough information to comfortably select a firewall to protect your home computer or home computer network.

11.5.1 What Firewalls Can and Can't Do

Firewalls can protect against hackers and enforce security policies. However, they *can't* make you behave and they can't protect against embedded attacks.

Firewalls Protect Against Hackers

An "intrusion" occurs when an attacker takes over your computer system. Many different techniques are used to hijack systems this way. Hackers might break into your system to leisurely poke around your files and read personal data; they might use your resources, launch a denial-of-service (DoS) attack, or steal your personal or financial information. Firewalls can help to protect you against many of these attacks by keeping you aware of when an outside program tries to access your computer through its ports or a program running on your computer tries to access the Internet.

Firewalls Enforce Security Policies

Firewalls also enforce security policies to provide protection from inside out. The library has a firewall. Your school has a firewall. In each case, the firewall has probably been set to block access to certain sites. Your school doesn't want you to visit sites with inappropriate or obscene material. Your library has probably blocked access to free email accounts. Many libraries do this so that the computers intended to allow patrons to complete Internet research aren't always filled with people checking their email instead.

In all these cases, the firewall's actions represent a policy that was established for a reason. If you're behind a firewall and decide to try to figure out "a way around it," you know that you really shouldn't be doing that. What you might not know is that what you are doing might be logged by the firewall.

Firewalls Don't Make You Behave

Unless your neighbor's children are Stepford kids, you already know that just because the babysitter comes over doesn't mean the kids will behave. They may not jump out the windows, but that's not to say they won't be on the Internet IMing their friends 'til the wee morning hours. Like a babysitter, a firewall only has so much control. A good firewall will enforce the security policies it has been set to enforce. Usually, that means that it might block certain sites or prevent certain programs from accessing the Internet. What it won't and can't do is make YOU behave online. Your firewall has no say over what you type when IMing your friends, which types of sites you visit (unless they're specifically blocked), or what kinds of email you send. Those things, along with the rest of your online behavior, are the products of your choices, not your firewall.

> **"Firewalls are not in place to make you behave."**
>
> Marcus Ranum, inventor of the first firewall and the security expert who connected the White House to the Internet.

Firewalls Don't Protect Against Embedded Attacks

Firewalls also don't protect you against "data-driven attacks." These types of attacks are initiated by an attack tool or malicious code that you inadvertently download or receive as an unwanted email attachment. For more details on avoiding embedded attacks, please read Chapter 2, "Drive-By Malicious Code."

11.5.2 So What's a Firewall?

A **firewall** is a piece of software that protects your computer (or your entire home network) by controlling the type of traffic that's allowed to pass between two networks. In many ways, your firewall is like the lock on the front door to your house. Your front door lock keeps thieves, potential attackers, and nosy neighbors out of your house. By monitoring traffic to and from your computer and watching programs that communicate with your computer, your firewall performs much the same functions. It functions as the lock on your computer's front door to the Internet, basically either permitting or denying program requests to send data into or out of your computer or network.

> **Firewall**   A piece of software that controls the type of traffic that is allowed to pass between two networks.

Amazingly, many people don't know whether they're using a firewall. Some users actually have a firewall and don't even know it. If your home computer is networked, you may already have a firewall included in your router. A **router** is the physical device that routes information between devices within a network.

The major function of a firewall is to control traffic coming from or going to the Internet. On my home network, my Comcast cable modem is connected to my Linksys router. My PCs (yup, we've got a couple of them) then connect to the Internet through that Linksys router. From the Internet, the only device that can be seen is the router. My home computers are in effect "hiding behind" that router. The router passes along (i.e., "routes") all information going to and from the Internet. In no way can information get to or from any computer in my house without passing through the router.

Because a router can protect the machines it routes data to, the router functions like a grand entrance way. That makes it a logical position for a firewall.

Of course, the router is not the ONLY place you'll want a firewall. You should also have firewall on the PC itself. This kind of firewall is often called a *personal firewall*. [If you're using a dial-up connection, you won't have a router firewall (or a router for that matter!). Therefore, you MUST have a firewall on your PC.] Even if you have a firewall on your router, you should also use a personal firewall. The personal firewall will allow you to monitor the applications running on your computer and restrict when and if those programs are allowed to send data to or from your computer. Using a personal firewall also provides a second layer of protection just in case a hacker compromises the firewall on your router. With only the router firewall, a hacker who compromises the router firewall can easily access any computers connected to that router. Add a personal firewall and that hacker has only made his way through your first line of defense.

> **Router**   The physical device that routes information between devices within a network.

11.5.3 The Broadband Router

For the first layer of defense from the Internet, a firewall needs to be at the point where the Internet connects to your computer—that connection point is at your router. Another feature that is important is Network Address Translation (NAT). NAT allows you to use

> **Router Shopping List**
> - Network Address Translation
> - Built-in firewall
> - Wireless capability

different IP addresses externally from what you use internally. This helps to conceal your internal network, letting your home computer(s) "hide" behind your router. We talked earlier in this chapter about how your ISP assigns you an external IP address. A NAT router takes that assigned IP address and then distributes its own internal IP address to the computer(s) inside your home network. From the Internet, only the router's address is viewable. Because the NAT router assigns its own internal IP addresses, the IP address of your computer(s) remains private.

NAT Router   A router that uses Network Address Translation to keep the IP address of your computer private and unviewable from the Internet.

Like operating systems and major application programs, routers also have known security holes. Therefore, you'll want to apply any patches or updates as needed. For most routers, you will need to change the default login and password, default name, and make sure that the firmware is current. (For router recommendations, see Chapter 12, "Look Pa, No Strings!")

I realize that you will find many routers on the market. I really like the Linksys router because it's simple to install and administer, and it allows you to easily set up a secure wireless environment. Whatever your preference, make sure you bring your list when you begin router shopping. On my last trip, I asked the sales rep for a wireless NAT router with a good firewall. What I got was a blank stare and a shrug. Don't look for help from clueless people.

11.5.4 So How Do Firewalls Protect Me?

Firewalls have two major protective functions:

- They permit or deny requests to send data to or from your computer.
- They monitor port access requests.

Permitting or Denying Data

Firewalls either permit or deny data. This is called your *firewall policy*. It is something that you define. Some firewalls come with low, medium, or high configuration modes, which simplify the installation for home users.

There are two types of strategies you can choose from when setting up your firewall—a default permit strategy and default deny strategy:

- A default permit strategy means you configure the firewall to allow any host or protocol that you haven't specifically banned.

- A default deny strategy means you list specific protocols and hosts that are allowed to pass through your firewall. Everything else is denied.

You'll notice that there's a world of difference between these two approaches. While default deny is a more censored and potentially robust approach, it's also a lot harder to configure. Default permit, of course, is much easier to configure—you basically block out known dangers, adding new blocks as new dangers are discovered. While default permit is much faster to configure, this strategy isn't quite as safe as default deny. With default permit, you're basically allowing anything in until it's proven dangerous. With default deny, you're denying everything until it's proven safe.

Monitoring Port Access Requests

Firewalls monitor and regulate connections in and out of your computer by looking at everything that tries to access a port. You can configure your firewall to alert you every time an application or protocol tries to access a port.

Of course, ports that let data out can also let data in. Attackers often try to gain access to computer systems by first scanning for open ports. You also need to configure your firewall to monitor and possibly block inbound connections. Attackers know that home users often don't install firewalls and frequently leave ports wide open with vulnerable services running. If you want to learn more about ports and services, one of the best places on the Internet is Steve Gibson's site, GRC.com. Gibson provides details on ports and services, attacks and vulnerabilities. It's too much information for us to go into here, but if you want to really understand how ports, services, and firewalls work, I suggest you take the time to visit GRC.com.

11.5.5 Firewall Settings

Techies can dig down into the heart of a firewall and block specific ports or applications. Most other users, however, really prefer not to. Thankfully, most firewalls give you the flexibility to install quickly and easily by simply configuring your firewall setting to High, Medium, or Low (see **Figure 11.2**).

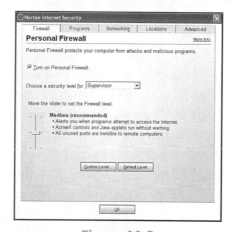

Figure 11.2
Norton's Personal Firewall

Which setting is best for you depends on what you do on the Internet. I strongly suggest that you start by setting your firewall to Medium security. If you need to, you can adjust the level down from there. ("Low" security is rarely a wise idea.) In my home, however, High is too restrictive, so we have our firewall set to Medium.

11.5.6 Free Firewalls

Want an excuse for not installing a firewall on your computer? Forget it. In recent years firewalls have become more powerful, much more important, and—equally important to many users—fairly cheap and often bundled into other security products.

If you can't afford a firewall, then download one for free. You can get the free firewall Zone Alarm from www.zonelabs.com. While it lacks some of the more

In or Out?

Microsoft's firewall only blocks internal connections—not outbound. That's basically half the job it should be doing. This type of firewall won't protect you from hackers who plant code that establishes outbound connections to watch your keystrokes and steal your data.

advanced features of its commercial siblings, it does the job if you can't afford to buy one. Zone Alarm also has a firewall that you can buy with more features than the free version.

Unfortunately, not all free firewalls do the job. One frequently used firewall that falls short is the one built into Microsoft XP. This firewall only blocks incoming connections; it does nothing to block outgoing connections. Free does not always mean it's good.

If this is ALL you have for now, go ahead and configure it. But keep a thought to upgrading to a better firewall at your first opportunity. To configure that Windows XP firewall, you need to use the Windows Security Center included in Windows XP Service Pack 2 (SP2). If you plan to run Windows Firewall, disable file and printer sharing under the Exceptions tab (shown in **Figure 11.3**), disable any other exceptions you don't think you need (such as Remote Assistance and Remote Desktop), and then install another firewall as soon as you get a chance. For details on disabling file and printer sharing, refer to Section 12.5.2 in Chapter 12.

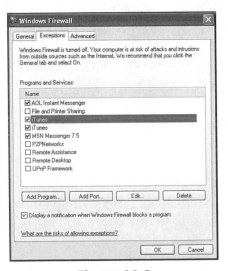

Figure 11.3
Disable Windows Firewall File and Printer Sharing

Look Pa, No Strings!

The Wireless Freeloader

Thirteen-year-old Michael was on cloud nine when he walked out of Best Buy with his new laptop. Top speed, top features, great price, and—even better—already wireless enabled.

Before he even got home with it, Michael stopped at his friend Juan's house. Seconds after walking in the door, Michael was on the Net, courtesy of Juan's parents' wireless router. Same deal at his dad's house. Seconds through the door, pop open the laptop and straight to his favorite gaming site! Michael was an instant fan of wireless technology. Nothing, it seemed, could be easier.

Then Michael tried to connect to his stepmother's wireless network. No dice. Unlike his dad or Juan's parents, Michael's stepmom had taken the time to secure her wireless network. She enabled encryption on her wireless router. Michael was blocked. Right? Wrong. Michael hopped out on one of the neighbors' networks because they were broadcasting to the entire neighborhood.

Michael's stepmom was surprised to find him logged into MySpace.com. Like Michael's dad and Juan's parents, the people next door never bothered to lock down their wireless network. Michael was on in seconds.

Michael's neighbors didn't complain, only because they didn't know. They were still sitting at home, accessing their favorite sites, and completely unaware that the boy next door was literally stealing their bandwidth. In less than two hours, Michael had gone from an excited new laptop owner to just another wireless freeloader!

12.1 No More Strings

Perhaps you are one of the millions of people getting rid of those computer cables around the house. This is one reason why wireless home networks are popping up all over the world. They make it simple, and string free, to connect to the Internet from every room in your house—even your front deck or backyard. Wireless for connecting to the Internet is the wave of the future. If you are not riding the wave now, you will be soon. Today, it's almost hard to buy a new laptop that *doesn't* come with wireless built in.

Your wireless PC still needs an *access point* to connect to the Internet—you can't just connect to air. In my house, for example, our access point is built into our Linksys router. How secure your wireless network is likely to be, and how you go about making it more secure, depends to a large degree on what hardware you purchase and how you configure it. This chapter covers some of the essential things to do to secure your wireless network, such as enabling encryption. It also covers some optional things to do, such as turning off network broadcasting, that might help deter "nosy neighbors" but not a skilled or determined hacker.

12.2 What Is Wireless?

A traditional computer network uses physical wires, cables, and/or telephone lines to carry data between the physical devices (computers, printers, etc.) within the network. A **wireless network** uses radio waves instead of wires to transmit and receive.

Wireless Network   A computer network that uses radio waves to send and receive data.

Wireless networks come in various shapes and sizes. For example, there are mega-size wireless networks that include hundreds of square miles and provide wireless connections for major cities. A wireless network that size is called a wireless *MAN*, for *metropolitan area network*. In most cases, however, when we discuss wireless networks, we are talking about **wireless local area networks (WLANs)** or even wireless personal area networks (WPANs). Since not many people use the term *PAN*, those wireless personal in-house networks are also often called WLANs.

A WLAN (of any size) works by using a radio transmission standard called WiFi, and the IEEE standard is 802.11. WiFi stands for *wireless fidelity*. In really basic terms, when you are using a wireless network, your computer is sending and receiving data over radio waves.

IEEE, the Institute for Electrical and Electronics Engineers, is the international group that sets the standards used in most areas of communications. Their standards ensure that products made by different companies can still talk to each other. IEEE actually has several standards for WiFi-based wireless computer networks. Those standards include 802.11b, 802.11a, 802.11g, etc. You'll notice that there's a pattern here, in that all the WiFi standards begin with 802.11.

IEEE (Institute for Electrical and Electronics Engineers) The IEEE is a serious trend-setter, creating the standards for computer communications.

The WiFi standards set the rules for how much data can be transmitted at a time, what speed that data is transmitted at, how far the radio signal travels, what radio frequency is used, and how the communicating devices should handle interference such as walls, hills, and devices such as microwave ovens (see **Table 12.1**).

Table 12.1 IEEE Wireless Standards

IEEE Standard	Distinction
802.11a	This standard provides only half the transmission range of 802.11b, but operates in the 5 GHz radio spectrum, which is less crowded.
802.11b	Devices using this standard transmit data at 11 megabits per second and can send and receive data over a range of roughly 150 feet.
802.11g	Devices using this standard send and receive data over a range of 150 feet, but can do so faster—at roughly 54 megabits per second.

There are specific differences between the various 802.11 standards. Up to 2005, wireless b predominated but is now being overtaken by g, which is backward compatible with 802.11b and is widely used in homes and hotspots. Both b and g are available in most WiFi products. Any new laptop purchased has g and is backward compatible with 802.11b.

When a wireless network is in operation, it creates what is usually called a **hotspot**. A hotspot is the area in which you can easily connect to the wireless network. If you're running a wireless network at home, your living room is most likely a hotspot.

You are likely to find hotspots in most airports, many hotels, and nearly all Internet cafes.

Public places that offer wireless connections are also called hotspots. You are likely to find hotspots in most airports, many hotels, and nearly all Internet cafes.

12.3 You Are Not Alone

Wireless connections are spreading quickly around the world. While visitors to Seattle may still gaze in awe at the Space Needle, they are probably unaware that at its top will soon be an antenna that beams Internet wireless capability over a 5-mile-square section of Seattle. How big can wireless networks be? Microsoft's new wireless net is projected to encompass upward of 17 *million* square feet. Among its many capabilities, this wireless net will allow up to 25,000 simultaneous sessions! That means that 25,000 people could use the network at the same time.

Of course, Microsoft rarely does anything in a small way. Still, wireless networks can be even larger. Australian ISP Unwired, in conjunction with Texas-based Navini, is building a MAN-size wireless network around Sydney covering 1,200 miles and including 3.5 million potential users.

MAN (Metropolitan Area Network) A wireless network that covers an area the size of a medium or large city.

Because they are designed to facilitate easy access, wireless networks are especially vulnerable to attacks. Wireless hacking is already extremely common.

Why are wireless networks so vulnerable? Signals sent by your wireless device can be picked up by any device within your range. Hackers know this, and some even drive around—literally cruising the streets of commercial areas—searching for wireless networks. This is referred to as **war driving**. Those war drivers are basically just waiting for their laptops to pick up a wireless network. This really isn't much different than our friend Michael, the 13-year-old freeloading on his neighbor's wireless. (Michael, of course, didn't have to leave his living room, let alone drive around town—which is pretty good given that he won't get his driver's permit for 3 more years.)

War Driving   A popular hacker pastime. This is literally driving around town trying to pick up wireless networks.

As **Figure 12.1** shows, wireless networks transmit data in every direction. Using the right tools, a savvy hacker can detect that data. Without proper security on your wireless network, any other computer with wireless capabilities in your range can connect to your access point.

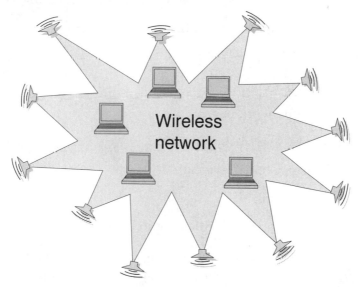

Figure 12.1
Wireless networks transmit data in EVERY direction!

As wireless networks multiply, so do the number of wireless freeloaders. A wireless freeloader is a person who uses someone else's wireless network without their permission. That connection might belong to an unsuspecting neighbor or to a nearby company with an unsecured access point.

Michael, the 13-year-old wireless freeloader, exemplifies how easy it is to connect to a neighbor's network. Unless you've configured security on your wireless network, your neighbor just might be freeloading right now. I don't know about your neighbors, but one of mine is a real jerk. I would rather not have him freeloading on my network or snooping through my traffic either. My network is just that—mine.

12.4 Locking Down the WLAN

To discourage war drivers and freeloaders, there are several essential and several optional steps you should take to lock down your router, the hub of your wireless network. Some of the steps are essential security measures and others simply help deter nosy neighbors and wireless freeloaders:

- Install the most recent firmware for your wireless router (critical).

- Change the router password (critical).

- Change the router LAN IP address.

- Turn off DHCP (if possible).

- Change the default network name.

- Restrict access to known MAC addresses.

- Disable remote management (critical).

- Enable encryption (critical).

- Turn off your wireless network when not in use.

In addition to connecting your computer(s) to the Internet, the router also connects them to each other. When information is "routed," it's being sent from one place to another, or more specifically, from one physical device to another. Thus, it's your router that forwards information between your computer and the Internet or between your mom's computer in her home office and the photo printer in your living room.

A traditional router moves your data by using physical cables and phone lines. Your wireless router instead routes information within your home using the radio frequencies defined by the WiFi standard being used. It may still use a phone line or cable to communicate with your ISP, however.

12.4.1 Downloading the Latest Firmware

Firmware is basically software embedded in a specific chip. Like your computer itself, the wircless router has its own firmware. Sometimes, hackers are able to get into wireless networks because of security holes in the firmware or due to limitations of the security features in the firmware. For this reason, it's very important that your wireless router has the most current firmware update installed. You need to check this, even if you're dealing with a brand-new router. For all you know, that "new" router may have shipped late last year and sat on a shelf at your favorite electronics store for months. So, the firmware may be out of date and the hackers may have detected new security holes since that router was originally produced.

Always be sure to check your router's firmware at the vendor site to make sure you have the latest version.

Always be sure to check your router's firmware at the vendor site to make sure you have the latest version. Check your router instructions to see how to connect to the router. Go to the vendor's website and look for the most recent firmware for your device. To perform the actual upgrade, follow the instructions provided by the company that makes your router. It is important that you only download firmware from the original vendor's website; do not install firmware from an untrusted third party.

12.4.2 Changing the Router Password

Like many important physical devices, your wireless router comes with password protection. Obviously, you don't want just anyone to be able to change your router settings and define who's allowed to use your wireless network.

When you connect your new router, it will have a default user name and password already set. This is usually something pretty obvious, such as user name **administrator** or **admin** and password **system** (some routers might not allow you to change the user name). Like you, anyone who has ever seen this particular router or the installation instructions knows the default user name and password. Since you don't want just anyone changing your router settings, you need to change those defaults immediately.

Default Passwords

Default passwords are a hacker's easiest route into your router and the rest of your home network. Always change them immediately!

Ideally, you should select complex words or phrases for your user name and password. Avoid using anything even remotely close to the default values. For your user name, also avoid using anything that's blindingly obvious. Your name, your favorite football team, the best online game you've ever played, and anything at all similar to the terms **admin,** **administrator,** and **system** are especially bad choices. For your password, follow the rules for selecting hard-to-break passwords that we discussed in Chapter 4, "Spy vs. Spy."

12.4.3 Changing the Router IP Address
Most routers have a default IP address of 192.168.0.1. Some routers will allow you to change the LAN IP address, which will make it harder for nosy neighbors to guess.

12.4.4 Turning Off DHCP (If Possible)
Disable DHCP if you can give static IPs to the systems on your network. If you know just how many systems you have on your network, you can easily assign IPs. If you need to have DHCP enabled, then you should limit the number of systems to what is realistic for your network size. I run DHCP because I have systems coming and going on the weekends, but I limited the amount of systems to ten (for more on DHCP, see Chapter 11, "Any Port in a Storm").

12.4.5 Changing the Default Network Name
This step can help deter nosy neighbors and wireless freeloaders, but you can't stop someone with the right hacking tools from gathering this information. However, anything that deters nosy neighbors and wireless freeloaders is still worth considering.

Every wireless network gets a name assigned to it called the *Service Set Identifier*, or *SSID*. Router manufactures set a default value for the SSID. When you begin to use your wireless network, every data packet you send on the WLAN will include that name (SSID) in the packet header.

When you're configuring your wireless router, you also want to keep in mind that most routers are set to automatically broadcast the SSID.

As it turns out, your wireless router can work quite well without announcing its presence to the world this way. So, it's really best to turn off the SSID broadcasting to deter wireless freeloaders. Determined hackers will still, of course, be able to find your wireless network by using tools to analyze wireless traffic.

12.4.6 Limiting Access Using MAC Addresses

The next step you want to take to lock down your wireless network is to limit access to only specified MAC addresses.

A **MAC address** (for Media Access Control) is a unique number given to each and every networked computer. The MAC address is hardwired into the network interface card (NIC) by the computer manufacturer. The NIC is also sometimes called an Ethernet card or just a network card.

MAC Address   A unique number embedded in the network card of every networked computer.

Your computer MUST have a NIC or you will not be able to include it in a high-speed network. Today, this really isn't an issue. However, it wasn't that many years ago when Ethernet cards were considered an unnecessary option for many home computers. If you've got some old computers lying around, you may very well even have one sans NIC that simply can't be connected to your network. Truthfully, though, any computer that old is likely to be too slow to be of any use on the Internet anyway.

MAC Filtering   A good way to deter wireless freeloaders by explicitly telling your router which computers are allowed to use your wireless network.

When you specify the MAC addresses of your home computers to your router, you are saying, "Allow in these computers and ONLY these computers."

This is a slight, but not a perfect, degree of security. Technically, MAC addresses can be spoofed. This requires greater technical skill on the part of your attacker. Still, limiting access to specific MAC addresses is one more thing you can do to make breaking and entering as difficult as possible and to keep your neighbors from wireless freeloading on your network.

To configure your router to use **MAC filtering**, you need to find the MAC address for every computer you wish to connect in your home network. To find the MAC address for your computer, do the following:

1. Click **Start**.

2. Click **Run**.

3. Type **cmd** and click **OK**. This will give you a DOS window, sometimes called a *command prompt* or *C: prompt*.

4. Type **ipconfig /all** and press **enter** (see **Figure 12.2**).

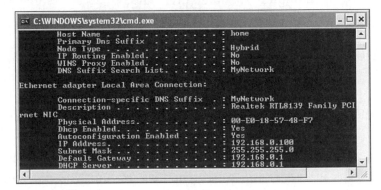

Figure 12.2
Listing the Mac address

You can see the MAC ("Physical") address 00-E0-18-57-48-F7 listed in this figure. Once you find your MAC address, go back to the user's guide for your wireless router and read the installation instructions on how to enter specific MAC addresses.

12.4.7 Disabling Remote Management

Some routers allow you to make changes to settings from a computer outside of your LAN. You should disable this unless you absolutely need this capability. Some routers already come with remote management disabled, but check to make sure.

12.4.8 Enabling Encryption

When you enable encryption, you're telling the router to scramble your traffic to keep unauthorized snoopers from making sense of any data they intercept. We talked about encryption in Chapter 9, "Safe Cyber-Shopping." In that chapter, we discussed the types of encryption used to protect online commerce. For wireless networks, three types of encryption methods are available, each using a different security protocol (see **Table 12.2**).

Table 12.2 Wireless Encryption Methods

Method	Description	Definition
WEP	Wired Equivalent Privacy	This is an older standard, fairly useless to protect you against today's hackers. If this is the best option you have available, you should update your router.
WPA	WiFi Protected Access	This encryption method uses the TKIP (Temporal Key Integrity Protocol) security protocol. While it is much better than WEP, it has some security shortcomings that may leave your data at risk.
WPA2	WiFi Protected Access 2	WPA2 uses the IEEE Advanced Encryption Standard (AES) security protocol. Currently, this is your best bet for secure encryption. However, it may never be an option for older devices.

If your router does not support WPA, check for a firmware update that adds the feature. If the device will not support WPA, you need to replace it with updated hardware.

Regardless of whether you opt for WPA or WPA2, you'll need to define a pre-shared key (PSK). The PSK is used to encrypt (and subsequently decrypt) data shared between your computer and the wireless access point (your router). To use encryption, you need to define that preshared key. For most routers, you will do that by providing a passphrase that the router uses to generate the encryption key.

A good passphrase, like a good password, should not be words in the dictionary.

For example, you might start with a simple phrase such as "school is out for the summer." Now, let's take it up a notch by replacing the o's with zeros and the e's with the number 3, the word for with the number 4, and then take away the spaces. Here's the result:

```
sch00lisOut4th3summ3r
```

12.5 Configuring Computers for Wireless Security

Good wireless security depends first on good general security measures. So remember:

- Keep Windows patches up-to-date via Windows Update.
- Run a good software firewall.
- Run antivirus and anti-spyware software. Keep them up-to-date.
- Use strong passwords on all accounts.

With those measures in place, specific wireless security measures include:

- Enable wireless network encryption to match your router's.
- Turn off File and Printer Sharing for each wireless network connection.
- Turn off your computer's wireless transmitter when you aren't using it.

12.5.1 Wireless Network Setup

Once you have configured your router, you can make the configuration changes to the computers on your wireless network. The Wireless Network Setup Wizard in Windows XP (Service Pack 2) helps to simplify the process.

To set up the wireless network, click **Start**, click **Control Panel**, click **Network and Internet Connections**, and then click **Wireless Network Setup Wizard**. The Wireless Network Setup Wizard dialog box appears, as shown in **Figure 12.3**. Now follow these steps:

Figure 12.3

Wireless network setup

1. Click **Next**.

2. Enter the name you wish to use for your wireless network. As with user names or passwords, pick a name that would be difficult to guess. For this example, I'm using the name Net4Linda4Me&Mine, as shown in **Figure 12.4**.

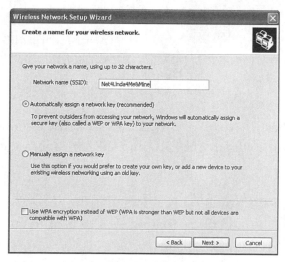

Figure 12.4

Wireless network setup

3. Click **Manually assign a network key.**

4. Select **WPA encryption** instead of **WEP** and click **Next.**

5. Clear the **Hide characters as I type** check box.

Type in the WPA passphrase into the **Network key** field and the **Confirm network key** field (see **Figure 12.5**). Click **Next.** The WPA passphrase should be a minimum of 20 characters. You can use up to 63 characters in a WPA passphrase. To avoid dictionary-based attacks, don't use common words, phrases, or personally identifiable information about yourself.

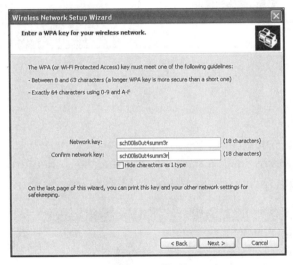

Figure 12.5
Wireless network setup

You can use a USB flash drive to save the settings and use it with the Wireless Network Setup Wizard to configure the SSID and WPA passphrase for other computers on your network.

12.5.2 Turn Off File and Printer Sharing

You should turn off File and Printer Sharing even to your home wireless network when you don't need it. You should *always* turn off File and Printer Sharing when you connect to any public hotspot. Even though this service runs behind your software firewall, you're safer still if you don't run it when you don't need it.

To disable File and Printer Sharing for a current wireless network connection, double-click on the connection icon in the system tray. (It's the one that looks like a single little monitor or PC, as shown in **Figure 12.6**.)

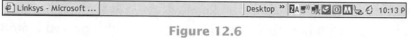

Figure 12.6
File and printer sharing

Click the **Properties** button in the Status dialog box that appears. Then, in the resulting Properties dialog box, uncheck the box for **File and Printer Sharing for Microsoft Windows,** as shown in **Figure 12.7**. Click OK and close both dialog boxes.

Do this for each new wireless connection you create.

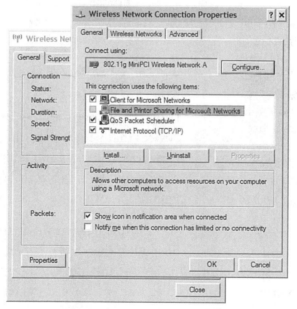

Figure 12.7
Disable file and printer sharing

12.6 Public Hotspots

As wireless technology continues to drop in price and surge in popularity, public hotspots are popping up in cafes, hotels, airports, bookstores, fast-food restaurants, and even in the air. Boeing is building aircraft with wireless access points. Imagine flying high with hotspots at 35,000 feet with WiFi-enabled laptops.

The big problem with public hotspots is that, for ease of use, they typically don't enable encryption. This means that hackers or eavesdroppers can read your traffic.

There are always dangers inherent in conducting private business in public hotspots. Because teens are among the heaviest users of this technology, they need to be especially aware of those dangers and take at least basic precautions to protect themselves.

Beware the Evil Twin

Malicious hackers are using a new technique, the Evil Twin, to tap into wireless systems. The attackers set their SSID to match the SSID of a public hotspot or a company's wireless network. Then, they initiate a denial-of-service attack against the "real" network, effectively taking it offline. Legitimate users lose connection to that "real" network and unknowingly pick up the evil twin instead. Sometimes this is called a *man-in-the-middle attack*.

12.7 PDAs and Mobile Devices

Laptop computers are no longer the only devices that people are using on wireless networks. You may in fact be accessing the Net on anything but your laptop—your PDA, Palm Pilot, or your cell phone.

Some of the newer mobile devices even combine all of the above. When I travel, I rely heavily on a Treo 650 smart phone. In this one tiny device, I get a cell phone, digital camera, web browser, email access, and organizer. I can easily get to any website, read my email, IM important messages, take pictures, and so on. Not surprisingly, I've taken to carrying my Treo instead of my laptop when I travel.

As I've come to rely more on my mobile, I've also become more aware that hackers are now beginning to target mobile phones and PDAs. Cell phones are especially attractive targets because so few users think about Internet security when they think about their cell phones.

But they should. Some pretty nasty attacks have already been launched at the cell-phone market. One such attack in 2004 appeared as a Trojan hidden in the installer in a popular video game that users download to their phones. Once installed, the game released a worm called Cabir on the phone. Thankfully, Cabir was fairly benign, spreading itself to other phones but not causing much damage when it landed. It did, however, have the nasty side effect of eating up battery life, leaving cell users stranded with prematurely dead phones.

Another Trojan, specifically targeting Nokia phones, Symbos Skulls, replaced the standard menu icons with a skull-and-crossbones icon. While the icon replacement was fairly harmless, this worm also caused most applications to stop functioning.

> ### Keeping Your Data
>
> Computer backups are a bit like flossing your teeth. We all know what we should be doing, but most of us fall short (at least occasionally) in execution.
>
> The next time you "suddenly remember" to back up your computer files, don't forget to back up your PDA. Like your computer, it probably contains important data (addresses, pictures, mini movies) that you really wouldn't want to lose forever.

> ### Security Tips If You Use Hotspots
>
> As emphasized earlier in this chapter:
>
> - Make sure your Windows patches are up-to-date.
>
> - Make sure your antivirus software is enabled and up-to-date.
>
> - Make sure you are running a good software firewall.
>
> - Turn off File and Printer Sharing for each new wireless connection you create.
>
> In addition, take these precautions:
>
> - Be discreet. Using your laptop in most hotspots is much like using your cell phone in the middle of a large restaurant. Be aware that your conversation might not be completely private.
>
> - Sending any private or sensitive information? Be sure the site in question is SSL-enabled.
>
> - Use VPN if you need to. If you have sensitive data on your laptop, you should use a virtual private network (VPN) when you connect to any network, whether or not you're currently sitting in a hotspot.

Warning!

Bottling up malicious threats to your PDA or cell phone requires vigilance, common sense, and protective software!

Like computers, which tend to use either Windows or Mac OS, mobile devices make use of operating systems. To protect your mobile device from attack, you need to know first and foremost which operating system it uses and check with your service provider to see if they are providing security software for that device.

Popular Mobile Operating Systems

- PalmOS
- Symbian
- Microsoft Windows Mobile (Pocket PC)

In addition to relying on different operating systems than their larger laptop counterparts, mobile devices also tend to use different communications standards. Most of today's mobile devices use a technology called Blue-Tooth to access the wireless personal area networks (PANs) that enable their wireless communications.

While PDAs are certainly at risk from malicious code attacks, they are also at physical risk in a way that other wireless technology isn't. Given their portability and cost, most users keep a close tab on their laptop computers. Those same users may not have a good grip on their mobiles. I've seen cell phones and PDAs left behind at schools, cafes, and restaurants. Many a user has also had a cell phone slip out of her back pocket and find its way into a friend's sofa or under a car seat.

To protect yourself in the event that your mobile literally slips into the wrong hands, you also need to set a hardy password to protect its contents. Don't make the same mistake as Paris Hilton. Never one to seriously protect her personal information, in 2004 Paris found her PDA's address book and photos had been posted to the Internet by intruders who'd hacked into her T-Mobile account and were apparently reading her email as well. How'd they get her password? Like many users, Paris picked a weak password. In her case, she chose the name of her dog. Of course, any person who's ever followed Paris' antics (on purpose or not) knows that Tinkerbell is near and dear to Miss Hilton's heart. Surely *you* can pick a much more secure password!

Chapter 13

Protective Tools

Do-It-Yourself Damage

Tim, a 16-year-old in Los Gatos, California, downloaded a write-your-own-virus toolkit off the Internet. Tim was getting into programming, and like most teens who write viruses, he was up for a new challenge.

With the do-it-yourself virus kit in hand, Tim was able to construct his own virus in record time. He didn't release it into the wild, of course. Becoming a black hat was never Tim's goal. He just wanted to know that he *could* do it if he wanted to. He wasn't really thinking like a bad guy.

That was actually the source of his downfall. If he really had been thinking like a malicious hacker, it probably would have occurred to him that viruses are pretty nasty bits of code. While his hacker toolkit made it almost embarrassingly simple to create his malicious code, it didn't tell him squat about how to get rid of the new virus.

The end result? The would-be hacker completely trashed his OWN computer system.

That's something to think about if you're tempted to try your hand at creating malicious code or even post a less-than-politic blog entry. On the Internet as well as in real life, you nearly always get what you give....

So far, every chapter in this book has started out with a teen security story. In addition to being true, most of those stories are about how easy it is to fall victim to hackers and malicious code if your PC isn't protected by the right security software.

Believe it or not, I can remember having a PC at home without using antivirus software. That seems like a lifetime ago. Today, I wouldn't even THINK about connecting to the Internet without antivirus software. I'd also need protection against spyware and adware, a firewall to protect my home network, and so on.

Since Michelangelo and other famous viruses propelled the concept of protective software into the public view, the tools available to defend home computers have become awfully diverse and complicated. In the past, you could get away with just a firewall. Then you needed antivirus protection, then protection against spam, then anti-spyware, then intrusion detection, possibly web filtering, and anti-fraud. The list gets longer each year. That's good for security vendors, but not so good if you have to buy licenses to run all of this software, and renew those licenses every year.

Before you start purchasing any security products, you need to understand which components are truly critical. Some security vendors offer bundled solutions—combining multiple products under one license. This is especially important if you have more than one computer to protect. Between the teenagers and adults in my house, we have six computers. No kidding! As your home computing power grows (and it will, trust me!), you'll want to simplify computer security. A good way to do that is to combine as many features under one license as possible. If the vendor you are using doesn't do that, then demand it of them or switch to another vendor. In this chapter, I'll talk about some of the companies and products you might consider to meet your computer security needs.

13.1 What You Need

There are essential security products that you MUST have in order to keep nasty code, and unwanted visitors, off your computer system. These are:

- **Patches**—To prevent problems before they happen
- **Antivirus software**—To keep new viruses from infecting your machine

- **Anti-adware software**—To protect you from both spyware and adware

- **Firewall protection**—To keep unwanted visitors at bay

- **Backup software**—To keep your files available, just in case

You'll notice that the first "tool" I've identified is more a procedure than an actual tool. That is, you don't so much buy patches as you make it a habit to apply them—or, even better, you configure your machine so that patches are applied automatically without you even having to think about them. I'll discuss, in detail, how to configure your machine for automatic updates in the next chapter of this book. For now, just keep in mind that applying patches is absolutely essential. Also, some people may argue that backups have nothing to do with security, but you must have a backup strategy to keep your data safe. Therefore, it's on the list for a good reason—your disk drive will crash some day.

Before you start purchasing any security products, you need to understand which components are truly critical.

For now, keep in mind that the actual tools I've listed here form an overall category often referred to as *protective software*. In a perfect world, you could run to Best Buy, walk to the aisle labeled "Protective Software," and pick up any one of a hundred perfect programs that would each meet every one of your computer-protection needs.

Unfortunately, life isn't that simple. The truth is that most of the protective software on the market includes two or more of the tools listed. Few, however, perform the functions of all five. Your mission is to find the right combination of products to perform at least five functions: (1) warding off viruses, (2) stopping adware and spyware, (3) closing up any known security holes, (4) blocking unwanted visitors, and (5) backing up your data.

Remember, some vendors bundle most (or even all) of these security solutions under one license. You may even be able to get all of these tools in one product in a way that meets your needs. This approach helps keeps everything under one license, which makes things easier to administer at home. You have to decide, however, whether the products being bundled give you all the security you need.

And, of course, you do often get what you pay for. The more robust and feature-packed packages are usually more expensive initially. For the long haul, only you can determine what it's worth to protect your computer, your data, your privacy, and your identity.

13.2 Choosing the Right Protective Software

While I've said—several times!—that you need to seriously consider purchasing a bundled approach, at the very least, you need to make sure that the solution you buy includes more than just antivirus protection.

Buying a bundled approach has a number of advantages. First, every security product you buy has a license. When that product is upgraded, you need to purchase that upgrade. This has a number of financial repercussions. Obviously, if you buy four separate programs to protect your machine, you're initially paying for four different licenses. (Even if you pick up your protective software as "freeware," you're still investing the time and energy to evaluate, select, download, and install those four packages.) Where this becomes even more cumbersome, and potentially expensive, is when you start looking at upgrades for all four of those products as well. In addition to the expense of paying for separate upgrades, you're also hit with the time factor of continually applying updates. With four vendors, it's unlikely that upgrades will be offered at the same time. You could be upgrading your virus protection in January, upgrading your firewall in February, upgrading your spyware protection in March. From a time perspective, this is simply too much work, especially when you have more than one computer in your house. Do you think for a moment that I update separate products for firewalls, virus checkers,

Know Your Vendor!

Choosing the right security protection against potential attacks is essential. Choosing the wrong software can leave your system open to attack. In some cases, choosing the wrong software can even initiate an attack. Several makers of free "adware" protection are really Trojans that actually *install* adware on your system.

spam filters, adware protection, etc., on all six computers in my house? To function properly, computer security needs to become second nature. It should not become a second job!

Another factor to consider when using multiple products for computer protection is that not all of the products work and play well together. In particular, you don't want to run multiple versions of firewalls and you *can't* run two different versions of antivirus software. (You really can't! While a virus checker is examining system files in search of any new infestations, it's behaving a bit like a virus itself. If you try to run two virus checkers on the same machine, they'll spend all their time complaining about each others' files with each claiming that the other antivirus program is potentially a virus. Kind of ironic, isn't it?)

To select the best set of solutions for your needs, you want to have a good look at the table on the following pages. What you're looking for is a combination of products that cover the features listed across the top with little or no overlap. You'll also need to consider one "feature" that I've not actually listed in the table—price. Much as I'd like to give you everything you need to make your choices, prices change much faster than this year's fashions. Any price that I included at this point would undoubtedly be wrong 15 minutes after I type it in.

One other thing that you need to consider before your purchase is that prices aren't the only things that change. Features themselves are a pretty mobile lot. It's entirely possible that a feature I've marked as missing from a particular product may be added at the very next upgrade. That upgrade may or may not come before we print, or you purchase, this book. Before making your final selections, be sure to check my feature list against the current features offered in the latest and greatest version of each product. It's possible that the vendor may have added a feature you are looking for after this book published.

*Note that in addition to those features listed, companies marked with ** following the corporate website also provide removal tools online for specific malicious code.*

Computer Associates (www.ca.com) **

Product Name	Anti-spam	Anti-virus	Anti-spyware/adware	Firewall	Phishing Protection	Parental Controls	Intrusion Prevention	PDA Phone
eTrust Internet Security Suite	Yes!	Yes!	Yes!	Yes!		Yes!		
eTrust Antivirus software		Yes!						
eTrust PestPatrol			Yes!					
Anti-Spam software	Yes!							

ESET (www.eset.com)

Product Name	Anti-spam	Anti-virus	Anti-spyware/adware	Firewall	Phishing Protection	Parental Controls	Intrusion Prevention	PDA Phone
NOD32 Antivirus Software		Yes!	Yes!					

F-Secure (www.f-secure.com) **

Product Name	Anti-spam	Anti-virus	Anti-spyware/adware	Firewall	Phishing Protection	Parental Controls	Intrusion Prevention	PDA Phone
F-Secure Anti-Virus	Yes!	Yes!	Yes!					
F-Secure Internet Security	Yes!	Yes!	Yes!	Yes!		Yes!		
F-Secure Mobile Anti-Virus		Yes!						Yes!
F-Secure Mobile Security		Yes!		Yes!				Yes!

GriSoft (www./free.grisoft.com)**

Product Name	Anti-spam	Anti-virus	Anti-spyware/adware	Firewall	Phishing Protection	Parental Controls	Intrusion Prevention	PDA Phone
Free AVG for home users (for updates and only one update allowed per day)		Yes!						
Anti-Virus Professional (more features and technical support)		Yes!	Yes!					
AVG and Firewall		Yes!	Yes!	Yes!				

Kaspersky Lab (www.kaspersky.com) **

Product Name	Anti-spam	Anti-virus	Anti-spyware/adware	Firewall	Phishing Protection	Parental Controls	Intrusion Prevention	PDA Phone
Anti-Virus Personal		Yes!	Yes!					
Personal Security Suite	Yes!	Yes!	Yes!	Yes!			Yes!	

McAfee (www.mcafee.com)

Product Name	Anti-spam	Anti-virus	Anti-spyware/adware	Firewall	Phishing Protection	Parental Controls	Intrusion Prevention	PDA Phone
Internet Security Suite	Yes!	Yes!	Yes!	Yes!	Yes!	Yes![1]		
VirusScan	Yes!	Yes!	Yes!					

1. Blocks unwanted pop-ups and ads.

Microsoft (www.microsoft.com)
One Care

Product Name	Anti-spam	Anti-virus	Anti-spyware/ adware	Firewall	Phishing Protection	Parental Controls	Intrusion Prevention	PDA Phone
One Care	Yes!	Yes!	Yes!	Yes![2]			Yes!	

2. One Care offers a two-way firewall.

Panda Software (www.panda-software-online.com)

Product Name	Anti-spam	Anti-virus	Anti-spyware/ adware	Firewall	Phishing Protection	Parental Controls	Intrusion Prevention	PDA Phone
Titanium Antivirus		Yes!	Yes!	Yes!	Yes!			
Panda Platinum Internet Security	Yes!	Yes!	Yes!	Yes!	Yes!	Yes!		

Symantec (www.symantec.com) **
Industry leader in security services.

Product Name	Anti-spam	Anti-virus	Anti-spyware/ adware	Firewall	Phishing Protection	Parental Controls	Intrusion Prevention	PDA Phone
Norton Internet Security[3]	Yes!	Yes!	Yes!	Yes!	Yes!	Yes!	Yes!	
Norton Confidential			Yes![4]		Yes![5]			
Norton AntiVirus		Yes!	Yes!					
Mobile Security		Yes!		Yes!				Yes!
Mobile AV		Yes!						Yes!

3. Anti-spam and parental controls optionally installed. Also provides vulnerability assessment.
4. Protects against threats at the point of transaction.
5. Also provides website authentication.

Trend Micro (www.trendmicro.com) **

Product Name	Anti-spam	Anti-virus	Anti-spyware/adware	Firewall	Phishing Protection	Parental Controls	Intrusion Prevention	PDA Phone
PC-cillin Internet Security	Yes!	Yes!	Yes!	Yes!	Yes!			
Anti-Spyware			Yes!					
Trend Micro Mobile Security[6]		Yes!						Yes!

6. Provides spam and malicious code protection for the Symbian OS, smart phones, and Pocket PCs.

Zone Labs (www.zonelabs.com)

Product Name	Anti-spam	Anti-virus	Anti-spyware/adware	Firewall	Phishing Protection	Parental Controls	Intrusion Prevention	PDA Phone
Internet Security Suite	Yes!	Yes!	Yes!	Yes!	Yes!			
IMsecure Pro[7]	Yes!							

7. Internet Messaging encryption protection, inbound outbound IM traffic protection, and spam blocker.

Additional Spyware/Adware-Specific Solutions

Product Name	Anti-spam	Anti-virus	Anti-spyware/ adware	Firewall	Phishing Protection	Parental Controls	Intrusion Prevention	PDA Phone
Lavasoft (www.lavasoft.com) Ad-Adware SE Plus			Yes!					
Sunbelt Software (www. sunbeltsoftware.com) CounterSpy			Yes!					
Tenebril (www.tenebril.com) SpyCatcher			Yes!					
Webroot Software (www.webroot.com) Spy Sweeper			Yes!					
Aluria Software (www. aluriasoftware.com)			Yes!					

As you begin to investigate these products, the first thing you'll probably notice is that I haven't listed anywhere NEAR all of them. Many vendors offer four or five different versions of protective software. For example, ZoneAlarm offers the following products:

- ZoneAlarm Internet Security Suite

- ZoneAlarm Pro

- ZoneAlarm Antivirus

- ZoneAlarm Anti-Spyware

- IMsecure Pro

This is true of most of the vendors I've listed. Keep this in mind if you find that you've covered most, but not quite all, of your computer protection needs. If, for example, you've got great protection already against everything but spyware, you might want to look for a spyware package made by the same company that's providing your antivirus and firewall protection. Two reasons apply here. First, there's a fair chance that they'll give you a better deal on the price if you already own one or more of their products. More importantly, though, there's an even better chance that their products are designed to work and play well together. After all, they hardly want to tie up their own technical support hotlines by putting features in their spyware package that don't work well with their own firewall or virus checkers.

> **Got a Preference?**
>
> Is your favorite security software missing from my list? If so, drop me a line at linda@ownURspace. net. Include your name, age, and address, and explain why you prefer the omitted product. You could find your preference, and yourself, included in the next version of this book.

13.3 Backing Up Your Stuff

One type of protection often overlooked is keeping backups. This could be because it often doesn't require getting new software, only a new mental outlook.

Several types of backup software are available. Your CD drive most likely came with backup software. If so, use it! If not, simply copying your important files to CD-RW could be all the backup you need. For heavy users generating a lot of files or space-hogging graphics, another option is to purchase an extra hard drive. Today's hard drives are small in size, large in capacity, and cheap. That's the route that I've taken at home.

What's more important than selecting a method is selecting a time and making sure the job is done. Since I have teens with active social lives instead of having my own, I usually make my backups every Friday after dinner. I make my work backups on Friday afternoon as well. It's a nice, calming Friday ritual that lets me know that I'm done for the week. Because I do it EVERY Friday, it also makes sure that the job gets done. Remember, it really doesn't matter how or when you make your backup copies, just so long as you DO IT and do it regularly.

If you keep important records online, say banking records or the college application essay you spent months on, you might want to keep at least one copy of your backup files at a place other than your home. That way, if your house burns down or floats away, at least you won't lose your files as well. (Incidentally, some people keep a home safe to store valuables and assume their backup disks will be safe in there as well. That's probably NOT the case. Remember the Ray Bradbury classic? Paper burns at 451 degrees Fahrenheit. CDs will melt at much lower temps. Your beloved collection of banned books might be safe in a traditional home safe, but that extra copy of your computer backups is probably safest out of the house!)

Don't forget! To be of use, backup files need to be fairly recent. How often that is depends on how often you use your computer and what you use it for. For most users, though, once a week is the absolute minimum. So, select a time and a method and start backing up now!

13.3.1 Spam Blocking

An incredible amount of malicious code travels via unwanted, unsolicited email. Blocking spam reduces your exposure to this code. It also saves you a lot of wasted time and general annoyance. Spam blocking is offered as a feature on many packages designed to eliminate spyware as well as in some antivirus packages.

13.3.2 SPIM Blocking

A first line of defense in blocking SPIM is turning on your "Buddy list." Not many vendors offered SPIM solutions at the time this book was published, but I expect to see more products soon, because these slimy persistent creeps just keep on coming. One company, IMbrellasoftware.com, does offer solutions. If you find any other freeware or good products for IM and SPIM, send email to linda@ownURspace.net and let us know.

13.3.3 IM Protection

IM is simply not secure. Anything you send out over IM goes out in the clear. I was just talking to Kaitlin, a high school senior in Clearwater, Florida. She asked if she needed to worry about viruses with IM. Yes! If you value your inheritance, don't use IM on the same computer your parents use for online banking. When you're looking at security bundles, look for products that will encrypt and authenticate IM. Also check that your antivirus software looks for malicious code in IM attachments.

Several of the nastier versions of adware circulating in 2005 made the rounds by masquerading as free spyware checkers.

13.3.4 Phishing Protection

Some bundled security software now offers phishing protection to make sure your personal and financial information is not being sucked out by the scum. Check your antivirus or firewall software for updates. If your old security software is not keeping up with the times, it makes sense to go with the package that offers the most bang for your buck. If your products are not offering these new solutions, ask why and move on to another vendor that does, next time your software license comes up for renewal.

13.3.5 Intrusion Prevention

Protecting your system with a firewall is one part of the puzzle, and detecting attacks and potential intrusions is another. Intrusion prevention software was developed for large corporations; however, intrusion protection software is now being bundled by several companies for consumers.

13.3.6 Email and File Encryption

One of the best free tools on the Internet to encrypt email is from pgp.com. PGP stands for pretty good privacy. The problem is you need the other people who you correspond with to use it, too. Remember: When you send something through email, it goes out in the clear. Don't ever send anything through email you would mind showing up on the front page of the *New York Times*. There are several file encryption programs, and XP even comes with its own file encryption; however, you better be real smart about how you use file encryption, because if you lose the key you lose your files. Check Google for file encryption and you will find a lot of shareware packages out there—but be careful!

13.3.7 Pop-Up Blockers

Several of the nastier versions of adware circulating in 2005 made the rounds by masquerading as free spyware checkers. Although these versions had little in common (they were made by different people/companies, even originating in different countries), what they all shared was that they all nabbed users by showing up as pop-up windows (often disguised to look like system messages coming from Windows itself). Having read this far into the book, you are no doubt *much* too security-savvy to fall for this particular trick. However, if you share a computer with a younger sibling or less security-conscious classmates, you could easily fall victim to this ruse. Blocking pop-ups is a great way to eliminate that risk. Pop-up blocking is offered as a feature on many anti-spyware packages, and within Windows itself.

13.3.8 Removal Tools

Removal tools aren't technically "defensive" tools, but unfortunately defense doesn't always protect your system. Sometimes, you also need to clean up the mess when your computer protection fails. While it's best—and easiest—to think first and keep malicious code off your computer, you also need to know what to do when that fails.

> *If you use the Internet often enough and long enough, you're bound to get hit with something you're not prepared for.*

If you use the Internet often enough and long enough, you're bound to get hit with something you're not prepared for. Everyone does. One day, not long ago, my 13-year-old, Eric, came home from school and told me he had the Vundo.B virus on his system. Pretty scary, isn't it? You're probably wondering how on earth you can protect your computer system when the security expert giving you advice is getting hit up with viruses on her own kid's machine. How'd it happen?

He got nabbed in the gap. Every time a new virus is released, there's a little gap between when the virus hits the Net, when it's identified, and when the antivirus companies have added protection against that virus. Remember our talks about virus signatures? Well, Eric got hit by a variant of the Vundo.B virus after it was released but *before* that variant's virus signature had been added to antivirus software.

If that happens, and your machine is actually infected by a virus, often the only way to get rid of it is to run a removal tool. If that's confusing, keep in mind that the point of your antivirus software is to PREVENT you from getting hit with viruses and to identify any viruses you may have been infected with. The antivirus software isn't designed to get rid of each and every possible infection you might get. That wouldn't be practical. Remember, there are over 100,000 pieces of malicious code out there, with new code and new variants being released daily.

Once Eric's machine was hit with the Vundo virus, it slowed down to a dead crawl. So slow in fact, that even Eric—a die hard gamer and persistent blogger—finally gave up and quit using the machine.

This is what we did to learn about this virus and to get it off Eric's system. First, we went to the website for our virus protection software. We're running Norton Internet Security, so we went to the Symantec.com site and looked for information about Vundo.b. The description of this virus came up right away. It turned out to be a Trojan horse, not a virus. Vundo.B is a Trojan horse that was designed to drop adware onto the computer. It was easy to see why it was sucking up all of the resources from Eric's system. Next, we clicked on the link provided to download the removal tool. Eric's machine was too slow to even use at that point, so we downloaded the removal tool on my computer and copied it to a CD. Then, we took the CD to Eric's machine, copied the removal tool to his hard drive, and executed it. To all appearances, his machine was back to normal. Just to be safe, though, we then ran a virus scan and I made sure his antivirus software was up to date.

So long as you're running a full-service antivirus package, this procedure should work regardless of what company provides your antivirus protection.

13.4 Keeping It Current

Regardless of which software package or packages you select to protect your machine from malicious code, it is absolutely essential that you keep that software up to date. By this, I mean two things: configuring automatic updates, and purchasing or downloading new versions of your protective software package(s).

13.4.1 Configure Automatic Updates

When you set up your protective software, you'll have an option to select automatic updates. Do so! Each time you log onto the Internet (or at a specific interval, generally less than a week), your protection package will go off to its website and check for any important changes. Let's say that a nasty new virus has been released and is wreaking havoc on the Net. Your automatic update should automatically download and install the new signature to protect you from that virus, even if you haven't tuned into CNN and aren't aware of how much danger your data is in.

13.4.2 Buy the New Version

For most software, yearly updates are minor changes that really don't make much difference to normal users. Updating your computer security software at each version is essential. The rules of banking are unlikely to change in the next 12 months. The methods used to attack computer systems are. For every security hole patched, it seems a different black hat is designing a new and different delivery method for nasty code. Don't kill a $1,200 laptop by skipping a $50 update.

Chapter 14

Tweaks

Don't Trash Your System

In the last chapter, you learned about some of the protective products you'll need to keep your data safe. Like Mario, you also learned the importance of backing up your system. Thankfully, unlike Mario, you learned that lesson without losing a good chunk of your family's photos!

You can tweak your system in many different ways. We covered some of the important ones here. A word of caution: Don't tweak your system without creating a good backup. You could make changes that you regret and have no way to go back.

In this final chapter, you'll learn how to "tweak" the settings of software you already have in order to improve the security and privacy of your system. It's impossible to cover everything here, but the steps listed will help. Those tweaks include the following:

- Creating user (non-Admin) accounts

- Patching operating system and browser security holes

- Using automatic updates to keep patches up to date

- Toggling ActiveX settings for your own protection

- Adjusting browser security settings

- Testing the security you've set

14.1 Put Someone in Charge

There are two essential defensive measures that any home user can take at no cost. The first is to install operating system patches. The second is to NOT perform daily operations with administrative privileges.

> There are two essential defensive measures that any home user can take at no cost.

If you're not sure who the administrator is, chances are very good that you ARE the administrator. If you don't know what that means, you need to.

14.1.1 What Is an Administrator Account?

Windows XP assumes that the world contains two very different types of users: ordinary users and administrators. For this reason, Windows XP allows you to create two very different kinds of accounts: user accounts and administrator accounts. The **administrator** is the person in charge. She is the only one who gets to install software and perform other specific "administrative" tasks. Every Windows XP machine MUST have an administrator account.

Administrator The person in charge of maintaining a computer system. Administrators have special privileges not given to ordinary users.

In addition to the administrator account, you can define a whole bunch of ordinary user accounts. Those users get to use the system, but aren't allowed to make administrative changes. For example, users can run software, but not install it. Basically, user accounts have fewer privileges than administrator accounts.

A privilege is a type of permission. Your account privileges determine what you have permission to do. For example, there are three basic file permissions: Read, Write, and Execute. *Read* means that you are allowed to look at a file. *Write* means that you can save a file. This also means that you can change it. If you have Write permission, you can change a file that you've read and then save the changed copy. Finally, *Execute* means that you can run the file. (This assumes that the file is a program file. This is also why program files are often called *executables*.)

Since your account privileges determine what you are allowed to do, it makes a great deal of difference whether you are using a limited user account or an administrator account. A common mistake that many people make is that they install their systems to use a single administrator account. Then, everyone in the house shares the same account. This can be dangerous.

14.1.2 Why Are User Accounts Good?

As you just learned, the more privileges your account has, the more things you have permission to do. This also means that any programs that run under your account also have more permissions—even if those programs are viruses or worms and you're not actually running them on purpose.

Because of the damage that can be done by malicious code running under administrator accounts, you should really use the Admin account only when you need that level of power. For example, when you're installing software.

When you don't NEED to be the administrator, you should be using a user account instead. This does, of course, have a few minor drawbacks. Any time that you need to install software, you'll probably need to click the Switch User button, and log into the administrator account first. However, this is really a pretty minor inconvenience when weighed against the possibility of having your entire system destroyed.

We talked in great detail about the importance of passwords in Chapter 4, "Spy vs. Spy," so I'm not going to repeat it here. I will, however, say you have to have good passwords on all accounts. Please read Chapter 4 for the details.

14.1.3 How Do I Create a New User Account?

To create a new user account in Windows XP, do the following:

1. Click on **Start**.

2. Click on **Control Panel**. The screen shown in **Figure 14.1** is displayed.

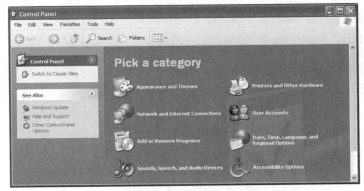

Figure 14.1
User accounts

3. Click on **User Accounts**. This displays the screen shown in **Figure 14.2**.

Figure 14.2
Creating a new user account

4. Click on **Create a new account**, then enter a name for your new user account, as shown in **Figure 14.3**.

Figure 14.3
Entering the account name

5. Select the account type. To create a user account (rather than an administrator account), select **Limited**, as shown in **Figure 14.4**.

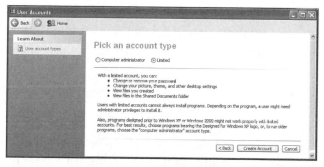

Figure 14.4
Account type

At this point, the initial User Accounts screen will redisplay, now listing your new user account. Wait! You're not done yet! Now you need to click on the account name to change the account by adding a password.

Ready to Take Charge?

Teens often make better system administrators than their parents simply because of the amount of time they spend using computers. The downside? Teens also use IM a lot more than their parents. Chatting with IM using an administrator account is risky. So is reading email, browsing the Web, and downloading. If you're planning to make yourself the administrator, be sure to create yourself a limited user account as well. It's really safest if you don't spend ALL your time as Admin!

14.2 Patching the Holes

At this point, it seems like I've said it over and over again: You open the box. You take out your brand-new computer. You connect to the Internet? NO! If you do this, it's just a matter of time before your data is stolen or destroyed, or your system is used as a launching pad for attacking other systems.

Before you start traversing that information superhighway, you must, must, MUST download any and all patches that you need to close up the security holes on your new computer. And, before you can even do that, you need to make sure you have a firewall installed on your computer or your router. [If your computer is networked, the firewall needs to be on the router that connects your computer(s) to the Internet. If your machine stands alone, at least for now, that firewall needs to sit on the machine itself.]

Installing the firewall before downloading patches is crucial. Otherwise, an attacker can make his way into your computer before you have a chance to download the updates and close the holes.

14.2.1 Who's Looking for Holes?

Apparently, more people than you think.

Obviously, companies that make software are looking for holes in their own code to prevent problems they'll have to fix for their customers. At least let's hope they are.

Hackers are looking for holes because that's just what hackers do. Some hackers look for holes because they're interested in destroying, selling, or stealing corporate data. Other hackers just like to cause annoyance without permanent damage, some have a serious vendetta against a specific company and want to use security holes to either embarrass or damage that company, and others do it simply for the challenge.

There are almost as many reasons to look for security holes as there are methods to exploit them. There are also some private companies that hire security experts and make it their business to look for holes. That is, they search for security vulnerabilities. Three of these companies are eEye.com, Secunia.com, and ISS.net.

There are almost as many reasons to look for security holes as there are methods to exploit them.

In theory, having professionals out hole-hunting seems like a really good idea. In practice, it doesn't always work out that way. One problem is that sometimes researchers who find holes report them to the public BEFORE the vendor has time to create a patch or to make that patch available for users. Of course, when I say vendor, I mean the company that makes the software that includes the security vulnerability. In some of those cases, the vendor and the public—which includes the hacker community—find out about the flaw at the same time. Hackers then immediately begin releasing attack tools that exploit the new vulnerability.

Very bad...

14.2.2 So How Do I Keep Those Holes Patched?

New security flaws are identified every day, so staying updated with the current patches is critical. The best, and only practical, way to do that is to make use of automatic updates. Beware of the fakes. Microsoft does not send patches in email notices. If you get an email from Microsoft telling you to install a patch, look closely—it's a fake. You have to download patches and you have to set your system up to automatically download patches. First, however, you need to make sure that your computer has Service Pack 2 (SP2). SP2 includes critical system patches that you must install before any and all other patches for Windows XP. Among other things, SP2 includes the update that actually provides the automatic Windows Update. No SP2, no automatic updates.

To determine whether XP SP2 is installed on your computer, do the following:

1. Click **Start**.

2. Click on **My Computer**. This brings up the screen shown in **Figure 14.5**.

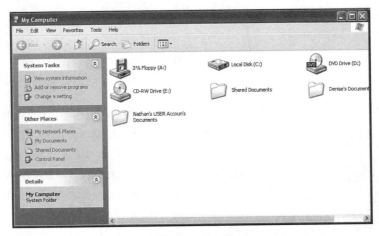

Figure 14.5
System information

3. Under **System Tasks** in the left pane, click **View system information**. If Service Pack 2 was installed on your machine, you will see that information listed under System, as shown in **Figure 14.6**.

Figure 14.6
System properties

If you determine that Service Pack 2 was NOT installed on your machine, you need to download and install that update from the Microsoft website *before* you can configure your machine to use automatic updates.

14.3 Using Automatic Updates

If you're going to run manual updates, the best day to do so is the second Tuesday of every month. Why? Microsoft announces new updates on the second Tuesday of every month.

> *If you're going to run manual updates, the best day to do so is the second Tuesday of every month.*

Of course, Microsoft also announces critical patches outside of the monthly window. Since an update for a serious vulnerability can pop up any time, I like to update my computer every day. On a manual basis, that would be a lot to remember and a bit of a pain. Luckily, I'm able to use Windows Update instead. This way, I don't need to remember to run updates and my machine is still kept up to date with the latest patches. [Note, however, that Windows Update does not work well with older versions of Internet Explorer (prior to IE version 5) and it does not work at all with many alternate browsers such as Firefox.]

If you're determined to run manual updates, you can do so at www.microsoft.com/updates. Your best option, however, is to go with the automatic updates.

To avoid confusion, be aware that there are actually two types of automatic updates now available from Microsoft:

- Windows Update
- Microsoft Update

At the very least, you should be using Windows Update. Windows Update provides patches (updates) for Windows XP itself and Internet Explorer. Microsoft Update provides patches for *all* major Microsoft products, including Windows XP, Internet Explorer, Outlook Express, and Microsoft Office.

14.3.1 Windows Update

Windows Update is the automatic update feature that provides patches for the Windows XP operating system. To enable automatic updates for Windows XP, do the following:

1. Click on **Start**.

2. Click on **Control Panel**. This displays the screen shown in **Figure 14.7**.

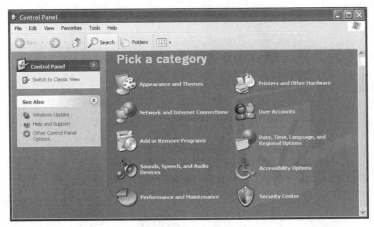

Figure 14.7
Control Panel

3. Click on **Security Center**. The screen shown in **Figure 14.8** is displayed.

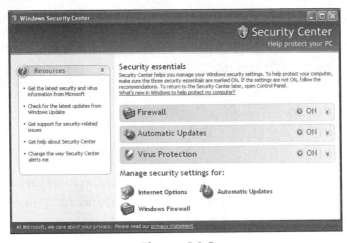

Figure 14.8
Windows Security Center

4. Check that **Automatic Updates** are set to **On**. If they are not, click on **Manage security settings for: Automatic Updates**. This displays the Automatic Updates dialog box, shown in **Figure 14.9**.

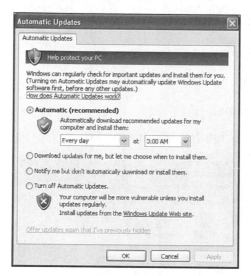

Figure 14.9
Configuring automatic updates

Make sure that **Automatic** is selected and enter a frequency and time for the updates to be downloaded automatically. I strongly suggest that you select **Every day** for the frequency. For the time, pick a time when you're not usually using your machine. I tend to stop my workday by 2:00 a.m., so the setting **3:00 am** was a good choice for me.

14.4 Keeping ActiveX Under Control

ActiveX was developed by Microsoft to make web pages more interactive. The way that ActiveX provides that interactivity is by directly executing small programs called *ActiveX controls*. Because ActiveX interacts directly with the computer's operating system, these controls are a favored place among hackers for sticking unwanted code. What better place to put attack code than in a program that will download and run automatically on many users' computers?

To avoid being attacked by unwanted ActiveX content, you need to adjust your Internet Explorer browser settings so that Explorer warns you whenever an ActiveX control wants to be downloaded. That way, you can choose whether or not to install that particular control.

To adjust your Internet Explorer settings, do the following:

1. Run Internet Explorer.

2. In the Explorer toolbar, click **Tools**.

3. Click **Internet Options**.

4. Click on the **Security** tab (see **Figure 14.10**).

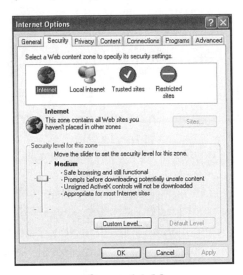

Figure 14.10
Internet Explorer Options

To disable automatic downloading of signed ActiveX controls, set **Security level** to at least **Medium-low**. I would recommend **Medium**.

14.5 Adjusting Your Browser Security Levels

In addition to using Internet Options to restrict ActiveX controls, you may wish to use this section to specify additional security details. If you're willing (and able) to put in the work, you can even use this dialog box to add sites you trust or restrict sites you wish to place off-limits.

If you add trusted sites, Internet Explorer will allow signed ActiveX controls to download from those sites without asking you first. Conversely, you can have Internet Explorer automatically reject ActiveX controls from restricted sites.

When selecting your final security level, make it as secure as you can possibly get away with. Try **High** first, to see if that setting will work for you. In some cases, it won't. I tried **High** for my teens but found that too many of their favorite websites simply wouldn't work at that level. After juggling a few settings, we finally settled on **Medium**. If you need to, you can drop down to **Medium** as well. Anything below **Medium-Low** is too risky because ActiveX controls will download without notification at those levels.

> **Note**
>
> The Local Intranet icon only applies if you're using a corporate network. You can just ignore that option.

14.6 Consider a Different Browser

Internet Explorer is used more than any other browser, with about 90% of the market. As you know, hackers spend time looking for vulnerabilities to exploit where they can get the most bang for the buck.

This is certainly true for Internet Explorer, as it is for Microsoft's web server platform, called *Internet Information Services*, or *IIS*. Serious vulnerabilities found in these applications have made it possible for attackers to plant code into vulnerable web servers. That code makes it simple for them to then transfer malicious code such as Trojans with keyboard loggers onto unsuspecting surfers' computers. The end result? Attackers might take control of your computer and simply install software without your knowledge. Exploiting browser holes certainly provides serious bang for the hacker buck!

How Your Own Browser Can Be a Risk

- Sending you to a malicious website without your knowledge

- Running malicious code or scripts (a series of commands to be executed) on your computer without your knowledge

- Redirecting you to a malicious website through a link in an email message

- Forcing downloaded code to automatically execute

- Permitting arbitrary code to run without your knowledge by allowing buffers to overflow

- Hijacking your browser settings

- Allowing your local files to be read by remote attackers

Try an Alternative?

If you'd like to try on an alternative browser, you can download one.

- For Firefox, go to www.mozilla.org.

- For Opera, go to www.opera.com.

To avoid this onslaught, consider using a different browser to surf the Web. Some of the alternatives to Internet Explorer are Firefox and Opera. Both of these browsers have strong security features, including spyware and adware protection, pop-up blockers, privacy controls, and automatic updates.

These browsers also use Java rather than ActiveX. Since Java applets are not integrated with the computer's operating system, it's much harder for hackers to use them to distribute malicious code.

Are these browsers completely safe? Not at all. They're simply less tempting targets at the moment. When the number of Firefox users suddenly surges, you will see a lot more hackers trying to attack Firefox. In the meantime, of course, you'll make a less tempting target with Firefox or Opera.

One word of caution—Microsoft does not play well with others. Windows Updates in particular doesn't support the use of Firefox. One solution might be to use Firefox for everyday browsing and use Internet Explorer for automatic updates. If you're using IE for anything at all, however, you still need to adjust those ActiveX control settings.

14.7 Testing Your Security

Once you install all of your security software, including your firewall, you need to test your security just to make sure. No system is bulletproof. Or eternal.

Diamonds might be forever, but security is pretty ephemeral. You might install the world's most inclusive security setup today, then have a new security flaw open up your entire computer tomorrow. That's why you can't just set it and forget it. The expert's mantra? "Configure security, test security, update security, keep your ear to the ground. Configure security, test security...."

OK, so it's not that catchy. But it is effective. And while it may not be 100% bulletproof, you'll at least have done everything humanly possible to ensure the safety of your data.

Several vendors have free security tests you can run over the Internet. These vendors include the big boys in security protection: Symantec, Computer Associates, and McAfee. My favorite site, however, isn't one of the major security companies.

Once you test security and you find something wrong, you need to figure out how to fix it. For example, you might have a risky port that is open and you need to figure out what the port is, why it's risky, and how to turn it off. We simply don't have enough space to go into every service and port, but open ports and risky services can open the door to bad guys. To test security, I am sending you to www. grc.com. This is Steve Gibson's site. I think his site provides a detailed security list, description of the risk, and recommendations on what to do when a test fails. Don't expect anyone to hold your hand, but if one of your tests fails, this site has enough information to help you figure out what to do, or at least get you started in the right direction in order to fix it.

If you've never tested security on your home computer, you should go to www.grc. com right now. Really, NOW! Click on Shields UP to get a quick look at how your security stacks up (see **Figure 14.11**).

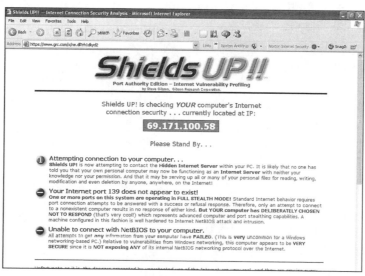

Figure 14.11

Testing security for free

A Check List for Mom and Dad

Congratulations! By allowing Internet access from home, school, or your local library, you've given your teen a private onramp to the information superhighway! With a few simple keystrokes, your teen now has access to encyclopedic knowledge, easy research for colleges and universities, and fast, reliable global communications. If you, like me, grew up just ahead of the digital generation, you're probably also still in awe of just how much the Internet really provides.

Hopefully, you've not also been caught up in the backlash—distorted media coverage that seems to ignore the multitude of cyber-achievements and focuses almost entirely on the dark corners of cyberspace. If your Internet savvy were based entirely on television news, you might think the Web was filled with nothing but phishers, posers, and potential molesters. Somehow, the billions of upright, honest netizens don't rate the evening news.

Still, the dangers exist, require knowledge, require protection, and warrant reasonable precaution. After all, you had your teen vaccinated against devastating diseases even though the odds of contracting polio in the Western world in the twenty-first century are much more remote than the odds of being phished online. It was a sensible precaution.

To protect your teen online, I recommend that you consider these sensible precautions:

- Be sure to fill your Internet Security shopping list: antivirus software, spyware protection, firewall, and patches.

- Realize that MySpace isn't going away. If you're concerned, sit down together and review your teen's MySpace page. Drill your teen and friends about not giving out full names, addresses, school names, or other personally identifiable information.

- Keep your teen's PC in an open space where you can see what's going on—not behind a closed bedroom door.

- Keep your family business in the family. If you have a wireless network, make sure you're not broadcasting your network to the neighborhood.

- Avoid webcams. (Teens are too often drawn to use webcams to post photos they may deeply regret in later life. Remove that temptation!)

- Don't be afraid to be the grownup. If you're concerned about your teen visiting inappropriate sites, install software with parental controls to block those sites. (Remember when you child-proofed your kitchen with safety latches and electric plug guards? Especially if your child is a young teen, it's OK to "teen-proof" the Internet a bit as well.)

- Don't be afraid to play the cop either if you need to. If you suspect your teen is doing something wrong online, strongly consider purchasing monitoring software. If your teen is doing something inappropriate, it's much better to be caught by a concerned parent than a real law enforcement officer.

- Don't forget to protect your own data as well. (Think of this as protecting your teen's allowance or college fund!) Particularly if your teen downloads software, music, or other items, you should keep your financial details and banking information on your own computer—not the one your teen uses.

- If your family shares a single computer, look into software designed to protect your financial transactions and personal information. Make sure you install that software if you're banking online or using your PC for other financial transactions such as online bill paying or shopping.[1] I do not recommend you use the same computer to do banking as your kids use to play games and download software from the Internet.

- Remember that applying patches to close security holes isn't a one-time "do it, forget it" thing. Black hats are notoriously busy little bees, so new security holes pop up continuously. Configure your system to use automatic updates to keep new holes patched.

- Remind your teen to think about the future. What teens post today will still be hanging around the Net years from now when they're working on developing real careers. Stupid comments and photos today can translate into unemployment in years to come.

- Keep it positive! With the right security software and sensible precautions, there's no need to be afraid of the Internet. Help your teen take advantage of the wonderful opportunities it provides, and you should too!

- Watch out for social engineering. Just because someone calls you on the phone and tells you he is from the FBI, it doesn't mean he really is! Verify it. Teach your teens not to give out any personal information over the phone, email, IM, and so on, that could identify their location or provide key personal information.

---

1. Norton Confidential is a good example of software that helps protect your financial information. It also has the advantage of being designed to work in tandem with the range of other Norton Anti-Virus security software products.

Index